Poetry Through a Lifetime

Part II

Later Years
1955 to Present

Brigitta Gisella Geltrich-Ludgate

AuthorHouse™ UK
1663 Liberty Drive
Bloomington, IN 47403 USA
www.authorhouse.co.uk
Phone: 0800.197.4150

Published by AuthorHouse 03/09/2017

ISBN: 978-1-5462-1346-8 (sc)
ISBN: 978-1-5462-1347-5 (e)
ISBN: 978-1-5462-1348-2 (hc)

Library of Congress Control Number: 2017911409

Print information available on the last page.

This book is printed on acid-free paper.

authorHOUSE®

This book of poetry is dedicated to the author's:

Mother, Ruth Margarete Geldreich, née Boehnke.
Father, Rudolf Karl Geldreich
Sister, Ursula Ingrid Kristensen, née Geldreich
Brother-in-law, Henning Holm Kristensen (husband of Ursula Ingrid)
Brother, Klaus-Peter Geldreich
Brother's family
His wife: Josie Geldreich, née Martinello
His sons: Michael Geldreich and Benjamin Geldreich
And his daughter:
Tessa Geldreich Mart
And
Tessa's husband: Jameson Mart
And their son and daughter
Archer Jameson (Geldreich) Mart
Arwen Isabelle Mart

Most of all this book of poetry is dedicated to the author's

Son: Douglas George Spencer Ludgate
And to
Spencer's father: Dr. Douglas George Pierce Junior Ludgate

Contents

Introduction

Poetry through a Lifetime, Part II, was written by the author during the latter years of her life from 1970 to present, as indicated by the timeline. Some poetry was upgraded in 2016, others were added in 2017. The author took to writing poetry first in the German language during the 1950s when she was a teenager, later her poetry became intermingled with English poetry, eventually they were written in English during the 1970s after the author's divorce and after moving with her son, Spencer, to Tucson, Arizona. From then on, the poetry has been written almost entirely in English up to the present day, some under the pseudonym of Max Davis, Max Douglas, and Bert Hower. For some of the poems actual dates of writing are available, for others only the dates of publication are indicated after the poem. It was an extremely busy time for the author and often the slips of paper with poems written on them went into the files without a date given. The time covered a period where many deaths in the author's family occurred: her godfather Hermann Geldreich (April 27, 1963), her grandmother (August 22, 1975), her grandfather (August 31, 1981), her father (October 6, 1981), her mother (January 7, 1989), her sister (October 2, 2001), and her favorite aunt, Rosemarie Gaupp (July 3, 2009). These deaths left behind a small family: the author and her son, Spencer, and the author's brother, Klaus-Peter, and his three children: Michael, Benjamin, and Tessa as well as Tessa's two children, Archer and Arwen.

The family passings are reflected in a certain way in the author's emotional makeup to write poetry. Also the author was working on her PhD, which caused much reading and research of academic materials, her move to Monterey to take up a position at a language school, and eventually her retirement. She had been in the workforce for close to fifty years. What affected the author mostly can be deduced from the timeline and at times from the notes given below the actual poems.

The anthropological poetry in the author's book *Stepping through Time* is listed in the back of *Poetry Through a Lifetime, Part II,* by their titles. There are 101 poems in that issue. These are not included in the current volume and if so only in a revised version.

Timeline Of the Author's Residencies
from 1940 to Present

1940	Moved from Kenya, British East Africa, to Italy, and from there to Germany and to Eastern European Countries
1952	Moved from Europe (Germany, Austria, Poland, Czech Republic, Switzerland) to Wallaceburg, Ontario, Canada
1952 – 1955	Wallaceburg, Ontario, Canada
1955 – 1962	Sarnia, Ontario, Canada
1962 – 1963	Findlay, Ohio, USA
1963 – 1964	Bowling Green, Ohio, USA
1964 – 1965	Perrysburg, Ohio, USA
1965 – 1967	Bowling Green, Ohio, USA
1967 – 1968	Sterling, Illinois, USA
1968 – 1969	Bloomfield Hills, Michigan, USA
1969 – 1970	Pontiac, Michigan, USA
1970 – 1975	Tucson, Arizona, USA
1975 – 1976	Oakland and Berkeley, California, USA
1976 – 1980	Los Angeles, California, USA
1980 – 1986	Carmel, California, USA
1986 to present	Monterey, California, USA

The Author's Life Adjustments
from 1970 to Present

The poetry covers certain life adjustments the author had to go through after her divorce in 1969

The author's divorce on March 29, 1969

The author making a life of her own together with son Spencer in Tucson, Arizona

The author studied toward a BA and MA degree at the University of Arizona, Tucson, Arizona, USA

The author studied toward a PhD degree at the University of California—
Berkeley, Oakland/Berkeley, California, USA

The author studied toward a PhD degree at the University of
California—Los Angeles (UCLA), Los Angeles, USA

The author took a position in Monterey/Carmel, California, USA

The author purchased a house in Monterey, California, USA

The author retired from the workforce on September 6, 2006

and

The author's former husband and reestablished friend,
Dr. Douglas George Pierce Junior Ludgate, passed away

Important Moments in the Author's Life Reflected in the Poetry

1955 – 1956	Adjustment to a life in a new country (Canada) on a new continent (North America).
1956	The author's engagement to Douglas George Pierce Junior Ludgate.
1957	The author's marriage to George Ludgate.
1958	The purchase of a house on Hunt Street, Sarnia, Ontario, Canada.
1962	The author's move to the United States where George Ludgate attended classes at Bowling Green State University.
	April 22, the author's godfather, Dr. Hermann Geldreich passed away. He was the next older brother to the author's father.
1965	The author's son, Douglas George Spencer Ludgate, was born in Bowling Green, Ohio, USA, on February 9.
1968	The author and George Ludgate separated in Bloomfield Hills, Michigan, USA.
1969	The author and George Ludgate divorced on March 29.
	In August, the author moved with son, Spencer Ludgate, to Tucson, Arizona, for the author to attend classes in anthropology at the University of Arizona.
1971	December 6, the author became citizen of the United States.
1975	The author graduated with an MA degree in Germanic Linguistics in June.
	The author and her son Spencer moved to Oakland, California, in August, for the author to attend post-graduate classes at the University of Berkeley, California.
	The author's grandmother passed away on August 22.
1976	The author and her son Spencer moved to West Hollywood, California, in August, for the author to finish her PhD work in Germanic Linguistics and Germanic Folklore at the University of Los Angeles (UCLA).

1980	The author moved to Carmel, California, in June, to take up a teaching position at a language school.
	The author's former mother-in-law passed away with eighty years.
1981	Oscar Wassermann, the author's grandfather passed away, August 31.
	The author's father passed away October 6.
1986	The author purchased a house in Monterey, California, and moved in on Christmas Eve.
1989	The author's mother passed away on January 7 early in the evening.
2001	The author's sister passed away on October 2.
2006	The author retired from a dean position at the language school.
2007	The author started to travel extensively: Bermuda, Yucatan, Los Angeles, Canada, Eastern Europe.
2009	The author's beloved aunt, Rose Gaupp, died July 3, in Schorndorf, Germany.
2013	January 18, the author published her first book, *Tales and Bedtime Stories*.
	May 9, the author published *The Muddy Little Bell: And Other Stories, Legends, Dialogs, and Essays*.
	November 18, the author published *The Lucia Rider: The Lucia Rider, The Island for Rent,* and *The Town's Child*.
2014	May 12, the author published *Stepping through Time: The Human Experience Poetically Reflected*.
	September 25, the author published *Fathers Can Be Good Dads: The Growing Relationship of a Daughter and Her Father*.
2015	February 20, the author published *Dance around the Treasure Box: A Novel Based on Conversations between Fred and Others*.
	June 21 the author's former husband, a good friend for the last nine years, Douglas George Pierce Junior Ludgate passed away in his sleep during early morning hours; he was eighty-seven years old and nine months.
	December 28, the author published *Two Summers of Adjustment: Novel*.

2016	April 23, the author published *The Little People of Oakcreek*.
	May 27, the author published *Cindy the Balcony Cocoon*, a children's book.
	October 27, the author published *Out of Balance*.
2017	March 24, the author published *Stories, Tales, Folklore, and Such As!*
	April 6, the author published *I am Jet, Jet the Cat*.
	August 23, the author published *Gedichte eines Lebens, Erster Teil (Poetry of a Lifetime, Part I): Early Years* (with English translations by the author); (published by AuthorHouse).
	Beginning of 2018, the author published *Poetry of a Lifetime, Part II*.

Poetry

1955 to Present

Wallaceburg,
Ontario, Canada

1952 — 1956

Wallaceburg, Ontario, Canada

(The author graduated from Grade XIII at the Wallaceburg District High School on June 26, 1955, and was on her way to take up a job as laboratory assistant at Polymer Incorporation in Sarnia, Ontario, Canada. At the laboratory she met her life-time friend Lilian Pfeiff, of former Latvian nationality.)

Lilian Greenshields, née Pfeiff, author's friend; photo by the author

1955

July 1955

Life-Time Friend

Her hair was golden.
It hung loose to her shoulders.
She was tall as I was,
And we became friends.

Today?
Years later,
We are still friends.

November 23, 1955

Peter's Christmas Gift

I am just a little boy
But still I love to live,
'cause Christmastime is full of joy
For ev'ry one who gives.
And now I give my little heart
To Mommy dear,
To Poppy dear,
To ev'ry one I love.

(Peter is the author's younger brother, Klaus-Peter Geldreich.)

**Klaus-Peter
Geldreich; photo by
a family member.**

Wallaceburg, Ontario, Canada

**(The author remembers a friend from school days at
the Gymnasium In Schorndorf, Germany.)**

1956

No other date than 1956

**Wolfgang Busch, the classmate from the Gymnasium in Schorndorf, Germany; photo taken
with Wolfgang Busch's camera; possibly a still (Wolfgang is an accomplished photographer)**

He tossed . . .

He tossed a crumbled-up paper note
To me when I joined the high school class.
He sat two rows over, more in the back.
Seldom did his missile miss me.

We came to Canada a few months spread apart
On the same ship to Halifax.
He settled in Winona, Ontario,
My parents and I in Wallaceburg.

We wrote letters; he came to visit.
We went together to Niagara Falls.
We saw an opera.

He waited on the road
For Dad to stop his car.

And then . . .

And then, I married George
And forgotten was my friend.
We did not meet again until
Years after, when both of us
Had lived another life.

(Author reminiscing her friend, Wolfgang Busch, from school days.)

**The author and her friend, Wolfgang Busch;
photo by Wolfgang's wife, Anneliese.**

Findlay/Bowling Green, Ohio, USA

1962 — 1967

Findlay/Bowling Green, Ohio, USA

(The author's godfather, Dr. Hermann Geldreich, the next older brother of her father, passed away, April 27, 1962. On February 9, 1965, the author's son, Spencer, was born in the early evening.)

1962 — 1965

The author's godfather, Dr. Hermann Geldreich; photo by unknown

No poetry was written.

Bowling Green, Ohio, USA, February 9, 1965

**(The author's son, Douglas George <u>Spencer</u> Ludgate, was
born early evening on Tuesday, February 9, 1965.)**

Douglas George Spencer Ludgate, born February 9, 1965; photo by author

Spencer and his mom, the author; photo by the author's husband

No poetry was written.

Sterling, Illinois, USA

Second half of 1967 to first half of 1968

Sterling, Illinois, USA

(The author followed her husband George with son Spencer to Illinois, where George was part of the original teaching team at Sauk Valley College, Dixon, Illinois.)

Second half of 1967 to first half of 1968

No other date than 1967

From left: George, the author, and Spencer Ludgate;
photo taken by a photographer, author purchased the photo

Teaching Team

We taught together,
You and I,
Sharing an office
You during the day,
I in the evenings.

You taught English
And whatever came

Along with it.
I taught German.

You and I
Were a teaching team.
And our son?
He was part of it.

Bloomfield Hills, Michigan, USA

Second half of 1968 — 1969

Bloomfield Hills, Michigan, USA

(The author moved to Bloomfield Hills, Michigan, 1968, with husband and son. In 1968 the author had to undergo exploratory surgery and shortly thereafter was separated from her husband, George.)

1969

November 2, 1969

As Autumn Gently Touches You . . .

Another bridge has just been spanned.
How many did you cross the years gone by
And still remained the one
As you once claimed to be?
Challenged by a world, senselessly cruel at times,
Confronting you with never-ending trials.
You wondered,
You searched,
And mostly hoped,
Seeking a promising tomorrow.

Tomorrow now becomes reality.
It offers fulfillment of the times
You said, "When I retire, then . . . "
Thus, cast away those binding shackles,
Take those heavy burdens
Off your shoulders,
Pursue the beauty of your innermost,
And follow all your dreams.

(Poem to the 65th birthday of the author's father, Rudolf Karl Geldreich, November 2, 1969.)

Pontiac, Michigan, USA

1969 to first half of 1970

Pontiac, Michigan, USA

**(The author set out her life alone with son, Spencer,
after separating from her husband, George.
She and her son lived on Patrick Henry Drive in Pontiac, Michigan.)**

Spencer Ludgate at Patrick Henry Drive, Pontiac, Michigan; photo by author

1969

No specific date other than 1969

Thank You!
**(A children's book, which was in the making,
for the author's son, Spencer, but was not completed)**

Thank you for the blossoms, white and pink
In spring;
For flowers full in bloom
In summertime.

Thank you for the colored leaves
In fall;
For crystal ice and fluffy snow
In winter time.

Thank you for a golden sun,
A sky so deep and blue.
Thank you for a moon and stars,
Sparkling in the night.

Thank you for the birds that sing
In trees that grow.
Thank you for the fish that swim
In lakes and streams that flow.

Thank you for my little pets,
The duck, the goose, the pony in the field.
Thank you for the frog and butterfly,
My faithful dog and playful cat.

Thank you for the house we have
In our little town.
Thank you for the land of ours
On our earth so big and round.

Thank you for the many toys,
Which fill my pretty room.
Thank you for my bed and chair,
The carpet and the curtains too.

Thank you for the food I eat,
The milk I daily drink.
Thank you for the beans and peas,
The tasteful bread and tender meat.

Thank you for the friends who come
And love to play with me.
Thank you for the laughter and the tears
I shed with them.

Thank you for my parents,
Whom I truly love.
Thank you for my sister and my brother
And those with whom I share
This great big world with me.

But most of all,
I'd humbly like to thank,
Dear God, for everything.
To him I'd like to say,
Thank you every day.

April 1969

Another Kite

Spring-like days! The wind is blowing.
Up to the sky, the kites are soaring.
Some fly high and some fly low,
And some, whichever way the breeze will blow.

Some kites, they fly so fast,
The strings are weak and seldom last,
And back to earth they will descend,
Most likely, somewhere high they'll end.

They land on roofs, they hang in trees,
Wherever one looks, that's where they'll be.

And to the little passerby's delight,
He points, "See, Mam, there is another kite."

Thoughts

My thoughts are free!

They ride the silvery clouds
And sail the stormy winds;
They touch the mountain crests,
And breathe the lofty air;
They cross the Seven Seas,
And roam all corners of the Earth.

No prison walls have yet been built,
No man has yet been found
To halt my thoughts
As fleetingly they speed
Through all the Universe.

Forever Mom

Mom, I love you because I just love you!
I brought you a frog. Look at his legs.
Mom, I'm right here in the mud.
Sorry, I got dirty and tore my pants.

I'm hungry, Mom.

Hi, Mom. I was on TV. Did you see me?
Mom, can I go to camp this summer?
I'd like to have a paper route.
Really, Mom, may I have one?
Mom, I failed a test.
I'll do better next time.

Mom, there's that prom . . .
I'll wash the car for you tomorrow.
Mom, I just can't today.
Sorry you don't feel well.
Take care of yourself, Mom.
Mom, I'm so busy with my studies.

Mom, there's a nice girl I met.
You want to meet her? Oh, Mom!
I'm married now.
Sorry you could not come.
But you know . . .
You have been ill, Mom?
. . .

Mom, we're going to have a baby.
Can you come next spring?
You really will come, Mom?
We're buying a house now.
Can you come in fall,
Mom?

Mom, you didn't write last week.
. . .

Who are you?
Where is Mom?
I only called to tell her . . .

Oh, Mom . . .

My Mother and My Father

My mother was a medic,
A doctor in the West.
I stayed with my father,
A rich man at the Bay.
He was kind and loving,
Caring all the way.
But I missed my mother
Living somewhere far away.

Then one day my father
Took me to see my mother.
I was to stay with her.
But when he rode out
On his favorite horse
With legs so white
And mane so black
I started to cry.

I cried and cried.
I wanted to be with him.
My mother and my father
Had decided on my fate.
I stayed six months with her
The other six with him.
I did not like the arrangement.
I cried an awful lot.

And then one day
I ran away.
I did not care whereto I ran.
It was my father who found me,
As I was hiding in a bush.
He held me in his arms
And told me he loved me much
But I had to promise
Never to run away again.

**The author's parents;
photo by the author.**

Pontiac, Michigan, USA

**(The author made plans to move to Tucson, Arizona,
in August to study anthropology.)**

**Spencer Ludgate playing with his building blocks on Patrick Henry
Drive, Pontiac, Michigan; photo by the author**

First half of 1970

January 12, 1970

The One Never Asked

Remember, Mom,
Sometime ago,
I used to be
My daddy's little man.
Now Daddy's gone.
He moved away
To love another family.
I know, I always be

Your big, big boy.
But tell me please,
Whose little man am I?

(The author's son's dilemma after his parents' divorce.)

June 11, 1970

Someone Said One Day

Someone said one day
Mankind invented God.
Could that truly be?
And then I must ask
Why God helped me
In so many ways?

He had me dug out of
A collapsed bunker
During World War II.
He prevented my son
From falling out of a
Gondola into whirling water.
He had my mother move south
With me and my sister
To escape Soviet armies.
He had me get out of a
Seizure while driving my car.
He had done so much more.
And now I am grateful to him.

I cannot believe that mankind
Invented God.
Mankind is not that wise
As God shows to be.
I thank God for everything
He did for me.

The Last Philosophy Lecture

We met,
You and I and all the others
Of the class,
To philosophize under the tree.
Thoughts flowing free
From inner minds,
As rippling waters
From their source,
Having a purpose,
Always necessary.
Seeking, wanting
Answers to their quests.
But where are these answers?

Minds are still searching
For a belief
That truly there is a God,
Who created a world
Not for deceit, but for love.
And in his creation,
Far more than dust,
And with a will
Man exists.
Thinking, hoping still.

His purpose so great
That you and I and all the others
Cannot understand
More than the need
That life must not be in vain.

(Dedicated to Mr. J. C. Harman, Community College, Michigan, USA.)

Elephantus (The Gray One)

Slowly he raises a heavy foot
And moves the wrinkled colossal
Forward.
He raises his trunk to protest,
But lowers it
Resigning himself to receive
His cheap reward—
A mere peanut!

Tiny eyes fill with water.
There are no wire fences,
Nor screaming crowds.
He only sees the land
Where grass grows tall
And trees shade like umbrellas.
For he cannot forget.

(Published in the March 1977 edition of *The Creative with Words Club*.)

His Soul (Long Gone)

In the valley below,
Pristine and calm,
Where uncluttered pastures rise
To lofty rocks,
A moment of his perfect life unfurls.

On his last stroll from home
Taking care of his health,
His health gently leaves him;
Caring hand tries to help
To bring him back.

But his soul has long gone,
Rising above the valley below,
Where green pastures rise
To lofty rocks.
But not as high.
As his soul will go.

(Published in the June 1999 edition of *the Eclectics!*)

Tucson, Arizona, USA

Second half of 1970 to first half of 1975

Tucson, Arizona, USA

(The author started university life in August at the University of Arizona, Tucson, studying toward a degree in anthropology and in Germanic linguistics. The author and her son lived on Rosewood Drive.)

Spencer Ludgate in 1970 before moving to Tucson, Arizona; photo by the author

Second half of 1970

Arizona Land

Arizona, land of sand,
Drought—oh, barren land.
Scorching heat.
Its only rendezvous
Torrential summer rains
Sustaining all there is.
"I have seen it,"
The foreigner exclaims.

"A hole in the ground—
Grand Canyon—
Yes, that's what
Arizona is all about."

But there is life in ev'ry ecological niche.
Gentle mountain meadows,
Host deer and bears in play.
Bees guard the entrance
To a grotto of a dripping spring,
While lizards, snakes,
And Gila monsters, horned toads,
Hares, chipmunks, woodrats,
Road runners, thrashers,
Quails, and wrens, coyotes,
Javelinas, mountain lions,
Are just a thimbleful
Of life that dwells in this
So-called forsaken land.

Life has been here
For countless thousand years.
The past of ancient people
No further lies
Than our stumbling feet.
Petroglyphs and painted rocks,
Pot shards, stone tools,
Household implements,
Mortar ground into a rock,
Native ruins,
Ancient ballparks,
Reminiscing those
Of dwelling further south,
All evidence that Arizona was
And is a land in which to live.

Today, there is a land
Stretching far beyond
Horizons' end—
Miles and miles of road,
Never quenching curiosity—
The travelers' thirst
To seek those wonders
Heard not once before.
Canyon de Chelly, Salt River Canyon,
Seven Falls, Saguaroland,
Monument Valley, Chiricahuas,
Organ Pipe, Walnut Canyon,
Wupatki, Sunset Crater,
Elephants' Feet, Balancing Rock,
Natural Bridge and dinosaur tracks.

If I could find a book
With endless pages to be filled,
And when the last page has been turned
Never could I even start to tell
The tale of Arizona land.

**Spencer in Saguaro National
Park on a cold desert
morning; photo by the author.**

Oh, to Belong

No one sees him,
As he labors across the park.
His crippled body aching
With every step he takes.
"Hi, Mister!" a little child smiles.

Another Falls

The moon stood half in the heavens,
And the wind drew clouds across.
A call at night foretells the coming fall.
One more time it calls,
The wild turkey.
Then the gun goes off,
And it is quiet.

October 28, 1970

Return

I don't know if I ever waited
Just like this before.
My heart beats faster,
As I watch the silvery bird
Rolling down the field.

It stops,
And then he comes.
My heart beats faster,

I can no longer speak.

It has been years
Since he has left our home
To start a life
Away from me
And our son.

Hatred grew, along with bitterness,
Until one day,
A letter came.
And in between its lines
I saw him reaching out.

And here I am.
He shakes my hand.
Silently I thank
The silvery bird,
Which brought him back to me.

(Inspired by a return of the author's husband.)

Foolish and Wise

There was a young man named Andy.
He lived in the land of plenty.
He spent lots of money,
Till he had not any.
The foolish young man named Andy.

There was a maiden named Betsy.
She lived in great poverty.
She saved every penny
Until rich with money
Was the wise maiden named Betsy.

November 1970

The Poor Student's Dilemma

Each time he walks along the street,
He looks and searches constantly
To find—maybe—a quarter or a dime.

And when he realizes
That just as poor as he,
There are hundreds more . . .
Each place has thoroughly been searched
By those who tread these grounds before . . .
Alas, he sees a dime.

It brightly shines, lying on the street.
He stops and reaches out for it,
But must accept that wheels
Of passing cars
Have firmly pressed it to the ground.

December 21, 1970

The Desert Star

The sun is burning the desert lands
Of the Navajos.
But as the cool night draws near,
A little Indian shepherd kneels,
Piously on open desert grounds.
His dark eyes full of hope.
A small herd of sheep
Nestled around his feet.
In the distance, mountains rise

And above all shines a light.
For here too in the desert lands
Of the Navajos,
Christmas has come.
A star so clear, so bright
Heralds in the most sacred of all nights.

(A Christmas greeting to the Minerals Department
Navajo Tribe, December 21, 1970.)

Pearls of the Desert

It lumbered its way across Skyline Drive
As the draft of my car turned it tumbling.
Struggling to get onto its feet.
I, in my dismay, stopped, stood puzzled
How to turn it over again,
The poisonous lizard of Gila.

The tire wrench became the probing stick,
When back on its feet, it continued
To lumber across the hot asphalt,
As I stood watching it, reaching safety.

(Published in "Dinosaurs, Dragons, Reptiles, and Animals of the Past," 1996, *Creative with Words Publication*.)

Haiku

Mountain waters flow.
Washes to wild rivers grow.
Out to sea they go.

December 24, 1970

No Hustle, No Bustle

It was two nights before Christmas,
And all through the town,
Not a gift to buy
Could be found.
The shelves in the stores
Were absolutely bare.

Not a single suggestion was there.
The mad crowd had bought
All the trimmings, all the gifts,
And on the eve before Christmas,
There was nothing left,
Except the ordinary.

No hustle, no bustle,
No last-minute shopping,
Were merchants still hoping?
From store to store,
I was rushing
In search of three Santas
Of chocolate so sweet,
But I found only one,
And he was no treat.
All out of proportion was he.
(I sure know,
Where next Christmas he'll be.)

Home I went
With my purse full of money.
Santas? I had found not any.
Lonely a bell was ringing on
Of a hopeful salvation man
For a generous passerby.
I sure learned a lesson.
All last-minute shopping
I must cease,
I better start early next year,
A month before Christmas,
Or maybe two.

(Based on "'twas the Night before Christmas.")

A Letter to Santa

Dear Santa . . .

It doesn't really matter
What toys you bring this year.
My parents say, I have too many anyway.
But, Santa, if you bring me any
Then make them please
A bike with training wheels,
A fire-spewing robot,
An erector set,
A sanitation truck,
Some roller skates,
A puppy and a kitten for my own.

And when you come, Santa,
Please note, we have no fireplace.
Don't slide down the cooler shoot.
It's all sealed off for wintertime.
But come around the house.
I'll leave the backdoor open there
For you at Christmas night.

Love, Terry.

**Spencer and his bicycle
with training wheels;
photo by the author.**

First Attempt on Christmas Day

Oh, Mom,
Don't hold it.
I can do it myself
Just let me go
And I'll show you.

**Mother's help is not
needed; photo with
the author's camera.**

Tucson, Arizona, USA

(The author was working at a branch of Kaiser Exploration and Mining Company, and attending classes at the University of Arizona in her free time. Spencer was enrolled in Lizzy Brown Elementary School, Tucson, Arizona.)

1971

No specific date other than 1971

Tranquility in Thought

The most inspiring thoughts
Reveal themselves to me at night
When moonlight meets the twinkling stars.
I see the vastness of the universe,
And feel benign tranquility.
My soul is swept up high
And merges with the All.
And for a moment,
I am free from earthly vile.

Summer Storm

Lightning is flashing
Over my scorched land.
Thunder is crashing,
As I look and stand.
And when the rain falls,
It washes the fields and land.
How tall now trees and crops grow,
As far as my eyes can go,
But how tall do I stand?

June 16, 1971

Mountain Phenomenon

A heavy crosswind blew
And through lights bright
And shadows sharp,
The mountains were disfigured,
Appearing baroque
In sculpture,
And even though miles away,
Seemed loomingly near
To the watching eye.

(See a revision of this poem, titled "Near or Far," October 11, 1971.)

June 21, 1971

If . . .

If I had money,
I'd buy a house
And fill it with love.

If I had money,
I'd ask all people
To share my house
Filled with love.

If I had money,
I'd feed my guests
And still their thirsts
And give them soft beds
In my house
Filled with love.

If I had money,
I'd buy the world
And fill it with people
Who have shared my house
Filled with love.

If I had money,
I'd buy the universe
And place in it worlds like ours
With people like ours
Living in houses
Filled with love.

If I had money . . .
But I don't.

August 24, 1971

I See a Color, Do You See It Too?

I see a color. It is blue.
Do you see that color too?
The sky is blue,
The sea and lakes are blue.
I see the blue eyes of my little girl.

And now I see a color. It is red.
The rose is red,
So are your lips.
And red are apples, big and ripe,
From apple trees you pick.

The yellow color now I see.
Yellow is the dainty butterfly,
The dandelion and the juicy pear.
And yellow is the silken hair
Of my little boy.

The color green can now be seen.
The grass is green.
The leaves of trees and shrubs are green.
And most importantly of all,
Green is the favorite color of my boy.

I have another color. It is brown.
The trunks of trees are brown.
The soil is brown.
But guess, whose eyes are brown?
Your eyes, of course, and yours.

And next, I see the color black.
Black are your winter boots.
Black are the tires on your father's car.
And every night is black
When you are sleeping fast.

And then I see a color. It is white.
The fluffy clouds are white.
The cold, cold snow and ice are white.
And white are all your pearly teeth
When you will brush them bright.

And last of all I see an arch.
It has so many colors.
The rainbow spans itself across the world,
And at its end I see
The prettiest color of them all.
It's golden through and through.

Do you see that color too?

(Published in the March 1976 edition of *The Creative with Words Club*.)

September 3, 1971

Haiku

Harvest time is near,
Gardens full with fruit abound.
Grateful is mankind.

September 10, 1971

Two Haikus

All day with his dog,
Grass growing high to his waist,
He plays in the field,

Chasing butterflies;
Never forgetting to bring
A flower to me.

(Dedicated to the author's son, Douglas George Spencer Ludgate.)

September 22, 1971

Haiku

Golden shines the sun
Over endless quiet seas.
A boat slacks its sails.

(Published in the March 1976 edition of *The Creative with Words Club*.)

October 8, 1971

Could It Be Spring?

A whisper rides on calmer winds
That everywhere new life begins.

Winter's final ice and snow
Have melted into tiny brooks,
Leaping, babbling over stones.

The chirping of a little bird
Heralds the coming of a warmer day.
Nature's beauty grows.

And in the fields and woods
Sprouting blossoms know no end.

Could it be spring?

October 11, 1971

Near or Far

With heavy crosswinds blowing,
Lights shining bright and shadows sharp,
The mountains are disfigured.
No longer dipped in purple mist,
They are baroque in sculpture.
Yet, many miles away,
Loomingly near they seem to be.

(Rewrite of "Mountain Phenomenon," June 16, 1971.)

Southwestern Autumn

Cows in man-made pastures linger,
Grazing in the sun of one more autumn day.
Wild turkeys call,
A thrasher echoing,
And through the Palo Verde tree,
Birds of melancholy sing.

The barrel cactus
In its desert realm,
An orange-golden crown adorns.
Grasshoppers clack their wings,
Flaming red they flash
Through mesquites still green.

But then the color wheel of autumn
Spins across the desert land,
And lingering green of summer
To golden amber wends.

Growing Up

I am free! Like the wind all around.
My hoofs barely touch the ground.
I shake my head, my mane flies high.
I kick my hoofs into the sky.
My heart abounds with glee,
For I am free.

But then one day, who comest there?
The trainer walking foals and mares.
He saddles up on mother's back.

Behind the two now I must track.
I shake my head, I buck a bit.
And in my mouth, the bridle hurts.

Every day, down the training way
I must walk behind the two.
Soon, this is not hard to do.
And when I pass the younger foals,
My hoofs I raise, my head I nod,
And proudly show them how to trot.

But once the evening comes around
And back to pastures I am bound,
I shake my head, my mane flies high,
I kick my hoofs into the sky.
My heart shouts with glee,
I am still quite free!

October 26, 1971

A Young Girl Remembering

I run through the meadow,
The grass growing high.
Flowers nod and greet me
When I pass them by.
There are white and yellow daisies,
Queen Anne's dainty lace,
Blue Bells ringing in the wind.
"He loves me, he loves me not," I sing.

I lie in the meadow,

The grass all around,
Birds and sky far above me,
I follow every cloud.
There are tiny sailboats,
With sails set in an endless sea.
I call to their captain,
"Wait for me, wait for me . . . "

I gather fragrant flowers,
Always two of a kind,
That none would be lonely
When in garlands I them wind.
And when I part from the meadow,
I gently bid it adieu.
Memories I carry
In each colorful bouquet.

(Published in "Nature, Vol. 1," 1995, *Creative with Words Publications*.)

Nail the Time
(A song: scores and music are available.)

Nail the time to the mountain,
Nail the time to the sky,
But never, never to the ocean,
With waves, it quickly rushes by.
    I am walking along the beach,
    Gath'ring pebbles, stones and shells,
    Dipping feet in cooling water
    I wish that time stood still!

Nail the time to the mountain,
Nail the time to the sky,
But never, never to the ocean,

With waves, it quickly rushes by.
    I am climbing one more mountain,
    One more top I just have scaled.
    Below me lies a valley green,
    Where peace still does exist.

Nail the time to the mountain,
Nail the time to the sky,
But never, never to the ocean,
With waves, it quickly rushes by.
    I am walking through the desert,
    Seeing life in barren land.
    Ev'ry plant enjoys its moment,
    Ev'ry animal as well.

Nail the time to the mountain,
Nail the time to the sky,
But never, never to the ocean,
With waves, it quickly rushes by.
    I am walking with my loved ones,
    And we understand ourselves.
    Soon we won't be with each other.
    Let us hold on to the time.

Nail the time to the mountain,
Nail the time to the sky,
But never, never to the ocean,
With waves, it quickly rushes by.

(Lyrics written by the author, music by the Broadway Music Production Company.)

Haiku

Winter's raindrops drum
Rhythmically on my roof.
Snug in bed I lie.

Pleading with Santa Elena

Little chapel near the border,
Standing on a rolling hill,
Painted white in its adobe,
Black through time its little bell.

Little chapel, may I pray?
May I pray inside your hall?
May I kneel at your altar?
May I see the sunshine fall
Through the paintings
Of your windows?

Little chapel, I cannot enter,
Barred by ocotillo's thorny crown.
Little chapel on the hilltop
Of a tiny border town.

(Inspired by the chapel of Santa Elena in Sasabe, Arizona.)

Tucson, Arizona, USA

(The author graduated magna cum laude with her bachelor's degree from the University of Arizona.)

1973—1974

No poetry was written.

Tucson, Arizona, USA

(The author graduated with an MA degree in Germanic Linguistics and Folklore from the University of Arizona.)

First half of 1975

May – June 1975

Tap Roots

Each tree, my child, has many roots,
Which twist and turn, and travel far.
But the tap root, my child, is here,
Where the homes of your people are.

(Published by the May/June 1975 edition of *The Back-Fence Reporter*.)

Oakland/Berkeley, California, USA

Last half of 1975 to first half of 1976

Oakland/Berkeley, California, USA

(The author moved with her son, Spencer, to the East Bay in order to study at the University of California, Berkeley, for her PhD in Germanic Linguistics and Germanic Folklore. Spencer enrolled in the St. Cyril School. The author's grandmother and Spencer's great-grandmother, Martha Marie Wassermann, divorced Boehnke, née Belser, passed away August 22, 1975.)

The author's grandmother, Martha Marie Wassermann; photo by unknown

Last half of 1975

October 1975

Autumn Morning

As I awoke this morning,
Autumn had come overnight
With colorful brushes
Had painted my garden bright.

(Published in the October 1975 issue of *The Creative with Words Club*.)

Oakland/Berkeley, California, USA

(The author held a teaching-assistant position while studying Germanic Linguistics at the University of California—Berkeley. Spencer started to play the trombone, and did presentations at school performances.)

First half of 1976

Spencer practicing trombone playing; photo by the author

January 1976

Two One-Two-Three Poems

Snow,
It fell
On our house.

Golden
The sun
Sinks at night.

(A "One-Two-Three" word poem, originated by Brigitta Gisella Geltrich-Ludgate. Published in the January 1976 edition of *The Creative with Words Club*.)

Bring Meaning to My Word

I do not know this word
You just have said.
To store its meaning in my head
You must explain.
My mind was born not long ago.
It does not yet contain
The wisdom of the world.
And when you say a word to me,
You must explain it too.
I grow on words,
And on them form my life.
And you in every way
Must bring a meaning
To the word I want to say.

(Published in the January 1976 edition of *The Creative with Words Club.*)

Haiku

A child and a dog,
Friendship bounded forever.
Love will always be.

(Published in the March 1976 edition of *The Creative with Words Club.*)

Do I Deserve This?

He died for us.
He died for me.
What did I do
To deserve this?

I am a mere human,
Nothing more.
But maybe . . .
Maybe I need help
From above.

It's Easter! It's Easter!

I search my room,
I search my house,
And under everything,
Through every nook,
I look.

I search the cellar,
I search the yard,
Behind each tree
And under every bush,
I look.

I see it there,
Up in the tree,
The biggest nest of all,
And in it waits for me,
My Easter egg.

(Published in the April 1976 edition of *The Creative with Words Club*.)

What We Are

I look through the window of the world,
A special window it is indeed,
Stretched out in front of me
I see the world like it is.
Only once every year,
The window to the asking eye appears,
And bears an image
One claims not to be his own.

The worst brought out in all of us
Through selfish greed, deceit, and lust
Cannot be erased from the window's pane.

Even deeds of those who care are in vain,
For not enough of us try to make
This a world, where each and one of us
Has rights to breathe and live,
To feel and care and love,
Without one moment's fear and hate
That turns us into what we are,
Reflected in the window of the world.

Spring 1976

Dear Professor Penzl: Sound Unrest
(In the good Old-High-German times.)

"Here we go again," the diphthongs said,
As the monothongs raised their newborn heads.
"Out au!" commanded a new ō.

"Out ai!" cried a new ē too,
As the ou and the ei as well pushed through.
"But hold, complained the ē2 and ō
Already existing from times long ago.

Since Common German days they had been around,
Doing their thing, each as a sound.
"We are still here and insist to stay.
There can't be two of us, so go away!"

But the new ē and the new ō
As well as the new ei and the new ou
Had already shed their old coats of ai and au.
There was nothing else for the oldsters to do,
Then to disrobe too,
And show their true identity.

Oh, many-faced they were indeed,
Each carrying its banner in rage,
Not perfect yet in their early stage,
But each in agreement with its partner a.
The ea lived here and there for a while,
Followed by ia and finally by the new ie style.

The oa, hailing from the ō, followed suit, of course,
Not wanting to upset the balance of the vowel course,
Pulling the o up to the u,
And the a up to the o,
Abandoning ua in the higher land,
Finally, the uo took the standard stand.

"Wait," was suddenly heard the voice of eo,
"I fit in here somewhere too!"
"Hush," said the stylish ie,
"There is room, come move in with me."

And the old eo did its twist,
As it thought about that and about this.

At one time, it considered an io to be,
But then it settled down, merging with the ie.
The i-Umlaut became famous too,
Directly changing the a, but indirectly the o and the u.

There is one more sound, we cannot ignore:
The one of the last syllable, existing before.
Not waiting for a formal invitation,
The shwah moved in without hesitation.

(Inspired while the author was studying for a Germanic linguistics' PhD degree under Professor Penzl at the University of Berkeley, Berkeley, California, USA. Professor Penzl's comment: "Sehr amüsant. Vielen Dank. Darf ich mir Ihr Gedicht behalten?" ["Quite amusing. Many thanks. May I keep your poem?"])

I Am Coming Through

"Have your fares ready,"
The jovial conductor called.
And those out there,
Clustering like grapes
Upon the narrow ledge,
Struggled for their coins.
"Make room for the little lady."
Squeezing together and
Pulling in rotund stomachs,
There was room for her,
For the young man too,
And his dog as well.

"Have your fares ready.
I am coming through."

The conductor called,
Squeezing and pushing.
And the cable car
Churned up the hill
And then down,
Brakes screeching,
Were they burning?
And the people were laughing.

(Inspired by cable car rides by the author and her son Spencer in San Francisco, California.)

Upon Seeing San Quentin

My son is just a little one,
Counting up to ten.
We traveled quite a bit this year,
And having seen the Kingston Pen,
San Quentin, and the former Alcatraz.
He wondered, "Are behind those bars
Really women there and men,
Locked away behind iron gates?
Can they not run and play
As I do every day?"
I nodded, "Yes, that's how it is."
"Would you like living there?"
He wondered then.
"Not for anything in the world,"
Was all I said.
"Me neither," he agreed,
Putting prisons out of his head.

**Alcatraz in the San Francisco
Bay; photo by the author.**

(Inspired by visits to the Kingston Penitentiary in Kingston, Ontario, Canada, and San Quentin and Alcatraz in California, USA.)

Afterthought

That night when fast asleep
The child lay in his bed,
I thought about what he had said.
It was about crime and punishment.
We call ourselves be civilized,
But can we learn not from the indigenous
How to control members of our tribes?
From early childhood on,
They know what can be done,
And what the consequences are
When rules are disobeyed.
Guilty ones are ostracized,
Ostracized by the entire tribe.
No one to speak to,
No one who cares,
All alone.

When punishment is carried out
He's taken back—
Cleansed—into their lives.
Those committing further crime
Are then and there dismissed
Forever from all tribal membership.
With punishment like this,
Crime seldom goes that far.
But we, we have no clear-cut rules.
Offenders pay and serve their time,
And then upon release
They are ostracized.
They pay forever for their crime.

Malpractice, a Sore Lot Indeed

Malpractice suits is all we hear,
The patients are revolting,
And when the pain strikes anyone,
The doctors must resolve them.
    But large are their homes,
    And large are their fees.

Their education was not cheap,
And learning time was long.
For it the patients now must pay,
Can anything with that be wrong?
    But large are their pools,
    And large are their fees.

A sore lot of doctors indeed,
Feel their actions they must prove,
Because in case of human error,
A patient cashes in on doctors' goofs.
    But large are their cars,
    And large are their fees.

Back and Forth

Those who once were have-nots,
Now are haves,
Having money, big cars,
Wasting fuel.

Those who once were haves,
Now are neither nor,
Having little money, small cars,
Saving fuel,

So that the haves can drive
And spend more money,
And the have-nots can neither nor.

Where is the balance of haves?
Back and forth it swings,
The pendulum does not seem to stop.

Unfinished

For many years, you have taken me
Across this land from sea to sea,
From mountain tops to desert lands,
From greeneries to ocean sands.
But then one day as climbing high,
Your steady breathing went a-strigh.
. . .

Los Angeles/ West Hollywood, California, USA

Last half of 1976 to first half of 1980

Los Angeles/West Hollywood, California, USA

(The author moved to Los Angeles with her son, Spencer, to attend the University of California—Los Angeles (UCLA) for her PhD segment of Germanic Folklore. Spencer attended local public schools: Laurel Elementary School, and Bancroft Junior High School.)

Last half of 1976

No specific date given than Fall 1976

I Lost My Mate

I lost my mate,
My mate for life
Here in the Hollywood Hills,
And so I coo
My lonesome call,
Among the twitter
Of other birds.
I rest at night
Among the branches
In the trees,
Lining man's swimming pools.
And as the day
Approaches once again,
I coo and call and coo
For my mate for life.

(Published in "Fly Away," 1997, *Creative with Words Publications.*)

Double Tercet Reversed

Horn
Blowing
Melody
False note sounds
Distract
Band.

(Published in the April 1976 edition of *The Creative with Words Club*.)

Said the Woman to Jealousy

"Why," said the woman to jealousy,
"Why do you torment me?"
    "I want it so,"
    Said jealousy.

"Why the pain, the agony,
When I see someone's gain?"
    "The gain belongs to me,"
    Said jealousy.

"I work so hard, while others
Often not."
    "The rewards should be mine,"
    Said jealousy.

"I have no time to spend
With others . . . "
    "I only strive for my success,"
    Said jealousy.

"Could it be," said the woman,
"That others strive as much as I?"
  "Such thoughts concern me not,"
  Said jealousy.

"Could it be that others earn
Their gains because they're good?"
  "Those gains should be yours,"
  Said jealousy.

"Should I," the woman asked,
"Enjoy success of others?"
  "Your success, they should enjoy,"
  Said jealousy.

"Should I be grateful for all
What I have not . . . "
  "You should have more,"
  Said jealousy.

". . . and love all what
I have got?"
  "It's you, just you, who counts,"
  Said jealousy.

October 1976

There's a Lioness under My Bed

There's a castle in my town,
A big one,
With towers and drawbridge.

It's a beautiful castle,
Because I live in it.

There are monsters
In the courtyard,
Fire-breathing ones.
But when I catch one,
It says, "Croak."

There's a wolf on the balcony,
With sharp teeth.
It chases me,
But when I pet it,
It wiggles its tail.

There are buzzards
In my castle,
Screeching loud.
But when I feed them seeds,
They sing.

There's a lioness under my bed.
She growls at my feet,
When I get up.
But when I give her milk,
She gently purrs.

There are giants in my castle,
Great, big ones.
Two of them.
But I love both of them.
They are my Mom and Dad.

(Published in the October 1976 edition of *The Creative with Words Club*.)

Candita

My heart breaks,
The neighbor's child is ill,
And I weep.

(Form designed by Elizabeth St. Jacques, Canada. Published in the February 1977 edition of *The Creative with Words Club.*)

Los Angeles/West Hollywood, California, USA

(The author became interested in various poetry writing styles of fellow poets, and designed her own style the One-Two-Three Poem.)

1977

January 1977

Proud!

Thirty! That's your age,
You wish for twenty five.
Cheer up, when forty comes around
Thirty sounds just right.
Then fifty comes along
And forty was a lovely year.
By sixty you admit
That fifty was not bad at all.
And then when seventy has come—
If only sixty you would have.
So can't you see
That every year
Should be accepted as it is.
For when you reach
Eighty, ninety, or even more,
You're really proud of it.

(A revised version of "Getting Old?" included in *Stepping Through Time*. "Proud!" has been published in the January 1977 edition of *The Doer Report*.)

Fishing along the Sacramento

Shawn went fishing with his grandpa
Along the Sacramento River.
The wind was blowing
Waves upstream
Along the Sacramento River.
Boats toyed in their leisure way
Toward wider water beds,
But Shawn went fishing
Near the railroad tracks
Along the Sacramento River.
Two ducks were sitting
On a sinking dock,
Basking in the morning sun.
The fish came swimming by,
And Shawn went fishing
Along the Sacramento River.

(Published in the June 1977 edition of *The Creative with Words Club*.)

The Lonely Gargoyle

So, let it be known,
I am only made of stone
And fastened to the edge
Of a tall construction.
I have feelings.

I see the birds at day
Spread their wings,
And fly as far as I can see.

And I, no matter how hard
I try, I cannot get away.

I see the bats at night
Come flutter out at me.
I try to break away
For just a moment to be
With them feeling heaven.
I cannot move away,
And so I must stay.

I have a fear.
A fear of heights
In this tall construction
Which holds me tight.
And all I am allowed to do
Is momentarily shed a tear.

(Published in "Emotions: People and School," September – October 2004, *Creative with Words Publications.*)

**Gargoyle at
Roslyn Church,
Scotland; photo
by the author.**

Evening

When the sun starts to set
And the air cools from the sea,
Three foals gallop in delight
Outrunning each other
Of the three.

(Published in "Seasons, Nature, and Animals," 2004, *Creative with Words Publications.*)

Most Touching Moments

Most touching moments came
When the iron lady—
His iron lady—
Came to pay her respect.
    "I will move the place card,"
    He said, "so you and I
    Will sit side by side
    Before the eyes of God."

Most touching moments came
When his foe and friend
Of the past
Stepped up and touched him.
    "We will do
    Our friendly battle,
    Up there," he said.
    And the foe and friend left.

Most touching moments came
When the oldest son
Gave him a kiss
And a salute.
    . . .

Those are moments
We need to remember
Forever and ever
And all eternity.

(Published in "Education—School 2004," June - July 2004, *Creative with Words Publications*.)

Comparative Skies

When reddish strings
Announce the coming day,
Where faded suns
Must slowly rise,
There is another sky.
And there . . .
    A fanfare heralds
    Reddish purple glow
    When western days begin.

And when the sun
Must travel far
From one horizon to the next
Across the light blue sea,
There is another sun
Out there . . .
    A jubilating sun
    Climbing evermore
    Through endless depths of blue.

And when at night
A reddish sun
Sinks almost in the west,
Accompanied by colored clouds
There is another sky
Out there . . .
    Where sounding trumpets
    Underline the color wheel's
    Majestic spins,
    Turning earth and heaven
    Into endless color plays.

(The author's reminiscing sunsets observed while traveling at sea.)

**Sunset while traveling at sea,
photo by the author.**

The Land of Turf

It is an old tradition
Heating the house
With cut turf.

But in Ireland,
It seems to still exist.
The land is a turfy land
And harvesting of the
Black muck is customary,
To heat the house
When it gets cold.

Celtic Hallow Evens

Make the ricks well,
Was the call.
Thatch the roofs
And tie them fast.
The harvest moon
Is stalking once again
This dying land.
First day of winter
Summons sheep and cattle
From wilted pastures
To farmstead byres,
Fortresses from where
To conquer biting winds
And winter's icy throes.
Burning wood and cutting turf
Offer warming glows
In earthen hearths,
As all set out

The turfy land in Ireland; photo by the author.

Sheep in Ireland; photo by the author.

A pile of cut turf at Killeybegs, Ireland; photo by the author.

In this sweet
Moment of life
For a renewal of the self.

There Is . . .

There is a hooting of an owl
And a thumping of a hare.
There's a pecking in the trees
A chirping everywhere.
    Deedledee, deedleday
    That's the woodland's way.
    Deedledee, deedleday
    That's the woodland's way.

There's a splashing in the sea,
Lonely songs of the whales,
Flapping fins of happy seals,
Schools of fish, without a tail.
    Deddleday, deedledee
    That's the tune of the sea.
    Deedleday, deedledee
    That's the tune of the sea.

There's a vast distant land.
Watchful eagles circling high,
Rattlers shaking banded tails
And coyotes calling out at night.
    Deedledee, deedledest
    That's the sound of the west.
    Deedledee, deedledest
    That's the sound of the west.

There's a land rather near
It's a land full of hate,
Full of anger, full of fear,
All of it human made.
    Deedledee, deedleday
    That's the human way.
    Deedledee, deedleday
    That's the human way.

But . . .

In the city, in the park
On a bench or in the grass,
There's a smack and a smooch
Between a happy boy and a lass.
    Deedleday, deedledee
    That's what we like to see.
    Deedleday, deedledee
    That's what we like to see.

Los Angeles/West Hollywood, California, USA

(The author made her first trip back to Germany with a stipend to study one semester at the University of Freiburg in the Black Forest. Spencer stayed with family friends in Bopfingen, Germany. It is the hundredth birthday of the author's grandfather, Oscar Heinrich Wassermann, born June 12, 1879.)

1979

January 1979

A Series of Double Tercet Reversed

Clouds
Balling
Billowing.
Bulldozing
Winter
Skies.

Green
The sea
Raging storm.
Calming breeze
Sea turns
Blue.

Seeds
Sprouting
Bearing fruit.
Leaves tumble
To the
Ground.

One
Torrent
Summer rain.
Desert shows
Colored
Bloom.

School
Is out,
Vacation!
Summer fun
Ends too
Soon.

Wine,
Spirit
Consumption.
Deadly foe
Lulling
Drunk.

Gray
The sky
Howling winds.
Blizzard calms,
Fallen
Snow.

Snow
Dancing,
Shimmering,
Glistening
Christmas
Eve.

Rocks
At sea,
Sun basking.
Seals await
Calmer
Days.

Tears
Falling
Hugging arms.
Pain is gone,
Smiling
Face.

Joy
Festive
Partying.
Sincerely
Season's
Cheers!

Kite
Tumbles
Earthward bound.
Wind rises,
Flying
High.

Cracks
In soil,
Barren land.
Soothing rain
Not in
Sight!

From a Meadean Point of View
(Focus is Role Theory)

The I, the me, and the myself
You have always thought of being
Just one individual, namely you.

But each of these constitutes
A different phase of yourself.

Thus, the I is your response
To attitudes of others;
The me a set of attitudes
Of others assumed by you;
And the myself stands for that
What you have made of the I and the me
To be a uniquely individual—you.

(Inspired by George Herbert Mead, sociologist, who treated this idea in 1934 in *Mind, Self and Society*. The poem is the author's version.)

Hierarchy of Hate
(Elevator Lore)

On the first day, on the elevator wall appeared,
"All Blacks belong to Africa!"
On the second day: "All Whites go to hell!"
On the third day in apologetic tiny script:
"Where do we Orientals belong?"
The answer did not come,
For the Ayatollah Khomeini came.
And on the fourth day smeared across the wall
In flaming red, "Iranians go home!"
On the fifth day a call went forth:
"Deport the Shah!"

On the sixth day the American reply:
"You're all nuts!" was clear.
On the seventh day, the wall was cleaned.
But on the eighth day once again:
"All Whites are dogs!" appeared.

(Based on the author's observation while riding daily the same elevator.)

Ambivalence

Eat fat
To keep cancer away!
Don't eat fat
To avoid heart attack!
Don't drink alcohol
To save the liver!
Drink two drinks of alcohol a day
To keep heart attacks away!

Confusion sets in:
What are we to do?

One-Two-Three Poem

Smile,
Gentle smile
Upon your face.

One-Two-Three Poem

Sun
Bursts forth
Warm another day.

Redondo Pier

Brandishing the shore,
Lapping pillars of piers,
Driven inland by the wind
The ocean foams,
And in the surf
Children awkwardly leap
Like fawns after their mother.
Laughter of innocence
Echoes into a future,
Holding infinite promises.
And on the pier,
Crippled and old,
A woman is watching,
Wrapped in blankets,
Wheeled in a chair.
Her future spinning
Its last thread.
She can only look to the past,
Where in the brandish below
She sees herself,
Laughing and leaping
Into a life that promised her all.

(Submitted to *The Monterey County Post*, September 4, 1995.)

Those Rainy Days

The rains come heaven-sent indeed.
The soil has swilled its need.
But what about your backyard friend,
The neighbor stray,
The raccoon,
The opossum,
The horses on the pasture,
How to their need in rainy days you tend?

Last night, my heart was reaching out.
The neighbor stray for days has not been about.
The opossum, only one of them came.
The family raccoon,
The mother fine, the children fine.
The father, oh, the father,
He suddenly was lame.

And how about the horses in the field?
No place for them as from rain they yield.
There's no money to build them a barn
With warmth, straw, oats, and hay,
And every moment tender care.
I fear rain must do them harm.

So, as you struggle to save yourself from the wet
Think about the suffering backyard pet.
Put out an extra helping of feed,
And put up a shelter
On the porch,
A plastic-lined cardboard box,
With towels old.
The reward you'll harvest will be grand indeed.

(Published in the February 1995 edition of *The Monterey County Post*.)

June 1979

Back at the *Hofbräuhaus* in Munich

I went back to the *Hofbräuhaus*
In Munich.
This time without my partner.
He had gone to Hungary
To visit his mother.

"Give me a glass of beer,
Leberkäse[1] and sausages two.
"You want to eat
All of that by yourself?"
The waitress wondered.

"I eat in memory
Of my partner when
The two of us
Ate *Leberkäse* and sausages two
And drank each a tall glass of beer."

([1]Liver paté is meat cuts sliced like cheese.)

Carmel, California, USA

Second half of 1980 to 1986

Carmel, California, USA

**(The author has taken up a teaching position in Monterey, California.
The author's former mother-in-law—Helen Ludgate, née Maudson—passed
away with eighty years; her birth date having been June 10, 1900.)**

1980

June 1980

On the Way to Monterey

Beyond the plane's tipping wings
Sierra Mountains rise
Above a distant haze,
Their snow-capped grandeur
Unveiled to searching eyes.

A Beach for Everyone

Along the bay from playa to sand dunes
A pinkish beach welcomes
Those who seek leisure
Upon its silken sandy floor.

Man and child building castles,
Bathing, basking—hedging rushing waves.
Dogs sooth their paws, barking,
While horses trot along the surf.

Dune buggies roar, maneuvering
Past sunning, playing guests . . .
Jellyfish carried to shore,

Dying in the midst of life,
Abandoned by their hosting sea.

The Afternoon Bay

Haunting cries of the foghorn
Urge ships to return
To the shallows of the bay
Before threatening walls
Of dense fog
Roll in over the darkened sea.

At Sundown

Golden sails
Set in the evening glow
As last sailboats
Return to white-sanded shores,
Leaving an ocean
Rushing and drawing
Endlessly to and fro from the west.

**Sun slowly sinking into the
sea; photo by the author.**

Carmel, California, USA

(The author's grandfather, Oscar Heinrich Wassermann, passed away August 31, 1981, and her father, Rudolf Karl Geldreich, on October 6, 1981.)

1981

The author's grandfather, Heinrich <u>Oscar</u> Wassermann; photo by unknown

The author's father, Rudolf Karl Geldreich; photo by unknown

No poetry was written.

Carmel, California, USA

(The author lived with her son Spencer in a section of a house on Cabrillo Street in Carmel Woods. Spencer went to Carmel High School.)

1984

March 8, 1984

Indifference!

Oh no!
Someone hit a deer
On Highway One.
I don't know, if I can stop
The traffic as it speeds
From home to work
And work to home;
From awe-inspired man-made sites
To nature's more splendid shows.

Gentle eyes had ventured
From wooded knoll to wooded knoll,
In slender grace hoofs had bounded
Over empty lanes.

A flash of lights
From green to red,
A roar,
The road began to shake.
Fearful glances
Just one more empty lane . . .

Oh no!
Someone hit the deer
And never tried to stop.

(Published in the March 8, 1984, edition of *The Monterey Bay Tribune.*)

The Curtain

Last night, I went to a play.
What a night, what can I say.
The actors stumbled on the stage,
One forgot his lines,
The others out of tune,
And one fell on his face.

But the curtain, oh the curtain!
The curtain performed rather well.
It was a flop, this very play.
But the curtain saved the day.
And when I applauded at the end,
Not for the actors was my intent.

December 20, 1984

Early Beachcomber

Curiously it peeks from rushing waves:
What face, what deep brown eyes!
What brought it near to shore
Where waters pound the sand?
Catch a fish, you friendly seal,
Before the crowd of the day
Will force you back to slipp'ry rocks.

(Published in the December 20, 1984,
edition of *The Monterey Bay Tribune*.)

**Sea lion at Monterey Bay;
photo by the author.**

Monterey, California, USA

1986 to present

Monterey, California, USA

(Along with Hildegard Dinkelaker and Brigitte Olbert the author toured Russia and some of the Stan countries, such as Kazakhstan, Uzbekistan, and Tajikistan. In December 1986 the author purchased a house in Monterey on Lottie Street and moved in Christmas Eve. Spencer had moved back to Los Angeles to start working there.)

1986

No specific date other than 1986

The Bridge of the Gods
(Cascade Rapids of the Columbia)

Oh, coyote, can you not forgive
The greed and quarrel of your people?
Must you cause the fires
In our camp forever lie dead and cold?
Loowit, you rewarded for her indifference
And we must travel to her lodge
To kindle fires for our camps.
You gave her beauty and youth for it.

Oh, coyote! She turned on you.
And rekindled the fires of warring chiefs.
Phato of the North and Wyeast of the South
Competed for her admiration.
They tossed the earth to shake—

Oh, coyote, you intervened,
And the bridge to the gods fell.
Over its boulders cascade now

The rapid waters of the Columbia.
Phato, as Mount Adams, and Wyeast, as Mount Hood,
Have fallen silent under cloaks of ice and snow.

But Loowit, oh, Coyote,
Loowit as Mount St. Helens
Spews smoke and flames with passion.
You turned her into Tah-one-lat-clah.
She is Fire Mountain, keeper of the flame.

With what fire have you left your people,
Oh, coyote?

(Published in "Spoofing! Vol. III, No. 1," 1986, *Creative with Words Publications*.)

Sun God's Hasty Flight
(Creator of a Splendid Sight)

In the fertile valleys of Western land
Dwelled an Indian princess among her kin.
Sun God on daily flights from east to west
Stopped to gaze upon her every day.

No longer wanting to journey alone,
He carried her forcefully from her tribe,
As he fled, he stumbled in great haste—
Mount Diablo became the princess's plight—

Dead in the arms of sorrowing Sun God
He placed her on top of Mount Tamalpais,
For her to be seen there forevermore.

In his fall, Sun God had cleaved the mountains
Between lakes and valleys, valleys and sea.
In poured the sea and out waters of lakes,
Meeting and mingling in the strait of gold.

The Golden Gate Bridge and San Francisco; photo by the author.

Today, a bridge guards the golden gate
And where the waters still meet and mingle
Stands a city, tall and proud at a bay.

(Published in "Spoofing," Vol. III, No. 1, 1986, *Creative with Words Publications*.)

Christmas Eve 1986

The author's house on Lottie Street, in which she still lives; photo by the author

I Bought a House

I bought a house,
Bordering Pacific Grove,
It is small
But the yard is large.

I bought a house,
Not for me
But for the dog.
Sundance needs space to run.

I bought a house
By myself.
It was not easy
Being a woman.

But I got the mortgage
And now it is mine.
Well, now the bank owns it.
But I bought a house!

Monterey, California, USA

(January 7, the author's mother, Ruth Margarete Geldreich, née Boehnke, passed away.)

1989

The author and her mother at a happy Christmas time; photo by the author's father

The author's mother, Ruth Margarete Geldreich, née Boehnke; photo by unknown

January 1989

I Wrote a Book

I wrote a book
A book to remember
My mother.

She always slipped away
In the eyes of my
Father's family
And their accomplishments.

Now the book covers
My mother's poetry
And her writings,
And her philosophical thoughts
For everyone to see
How very smart she was
My mother.

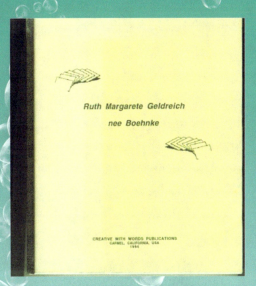

Ruth Margarete Geldreich
nee Boehnke

CREATIVE WITH WORDS PUBLICATIONS
CARMEL, CALIFORNIA, USA
1994

**Book on the author's mother;
photo by the author.**

Monterey, California, USA

(The author had to rework the yard on Lottie Street. It was mostly clay and nothing grew when she first moved in. She had to mold the yard with chicken manure tea and with top soil, every inch of it, hand by hand. The yard was large, a double lot. It was a lot of work, but it paid off. Her dog Sundance helped her in the process and so did a lady blue jay.)

1992

No specific date other than 1992

In My Yard

As I dug in the ground,
There was a chirp
And a cocking of head,
Looking for something to eat.

As I planted
Shrubs and flowers,
There were black paws
Digging them back out.

We had fun in my yard,
The blue jay and I,
But I chased the black lab
For doing the digging.

The Halloween Doll

Two dark eyes leered at me from
A dumping site.
"Please stop," a voice called so sweet
As I turned to leave.
"I was left here,
Abandoned,
No arms will hold me anymore."
"What can I do?" I asked,
Car keys jiggling in my hand.
"Today's Halloween,
I'll be condemned forever
To haunt dumping sites."

"That won't do," I said and turned.
I pulled her out from heaps of filthy cloth,
A doll once pretty in her time.
I washed her gently,
And dressed her up in brand-new frills.
A homeless child now holds her in its arms
As the child goes house to house with me
For a friendly trick or treat.

(Unknown when written by the author, possibly in Tucson, Arizona; published in "A Time for Seasons and Holidays!" 1992 by *Creative with Words Publications*.)

Monterey, California, USA

(The author had moved with her colleagues and students from an old school building in Pacific Grove to the Presidio in Monterey.)

1993

No specific date other than 1993

Sundance
(In memory of Sundance, the author's black Labrador Retriever.)

I bought the house for you, my friend,
A larger yard you need, to run and roam.
And run and roam you did, my friend.
You helped me plant shrubs and trees,
Unplanted flowers often times,
As fast as I put them in the ground.
You loved the grass, my friend,
To pull it out and eat it as a treat.
You rolled in mulch,
To keep away those ticks and fleas.
You guarded all, my friend,
Indoors as well as out.
But most of all,
You took such care of me, my friend,
As guard, protector, confidant—
As dear, dear loving friend.

And now . . .

And now, you're gone, my friend.
My heart calls out for you.
The yard is empty now, my friend.
The house stands silently bare.
And I alone amidst it all,
Wonder what I will do with it
Without you,
My dear, dear friend.

(Written upon the passing of the author's dog, Sundance; published in "Impossible Loves! A Return to Romance!" 1993, *Creative with Words Publications*.)

Love Tracks

She walks the tracks,
Five laps, ten, twenty-four,
Purposefully every weekend,
Early in the morning,
Saturdays and Sundays.

He runs the tracks,
Ten laps, twenty most,
Purposefully to burn off
Unnecessary weight,
Early in the morning,
Saturdays and Sundays.

She walks this way,
He runs that way,
Meeting in between,
Once here, once there,
While others walk and run
Anywhere.

Then one day,
She comes around the bend,
He had run the stretch.
In one swoop, he scoops her
Into the air and kisses her.
Slowly, bringing her down,
And runs that way,
As she walks this way,
Only momentarily slowing down,
Turning to look his way.

(Published in "Impossible Loves! A Return to Romance!" 1993, *Creative with Words Publications*.)

Monterey, California, USA

(Together with one of her colleagues the author went to an American military base in Panama City to teach a computer class. While in Panama City she toured with an eco-tour the Canal and the inland of the country's seaway.)

1995

February 1995

Panama
(Thoughts while Teaching in Panama.)

It's about to happen again,
A hotel room with a view,
The view that is,
Ships lying out in the bay,
Waiting for passage through the canal.

It's about to happen again,
The sun rising over the Pacific sea
And setting over the land.
Palm trees swaying in the breeze,
Hot days and balmy nights,
Busy people everywhere
As trade winds clear the air.

It's about to happen again,
A hotel room with a view,
The view that is,
Of a land which promises a
Greater tomorrow.
And as I leave the view
With heavy heart,
I know the greater tomorrow will come,
But the question remains,
In what way will it come?

(Published in "Nature, Vol. 4," 1995, *Creative with Words Publications*.)

Can I Forgive Him?

Can I forgive him
For being a hunter?
Can I forgive him
For clearing the neighborhood
Of mice and rats?
Can I forgive him
For having instincts?

I don't think that is possible.

But can I forgive him
For hunting baby raccoons
Or a baby opossum?
Both healthy, both full of life . . .
It is so hard to forgive him.
Had I not taken him in
Giving him a chance
When abandoned he came
To the neighborhood,
The black fuzzy coon cat?

**Blackie, the author's pet;
photo by the author.**

(In memory of Blackie, the black-haired coon cat mix, one of the author's pets; photo by the author.)

Gift of the Birds

We know she feeds us—
Indirectly possibly—
Nonetheless, she feeds us
With cat food for the neighbor's stray,
Breadcrumbs for the raccoon family,
Leftovers for the opossum bunch.
She feeds us all right.

We know she likes Christmas trees,
Young ones, she can plant into the ground
After the festive season is gone.
Her backyard has a fence already
Of Christmas trees, staggering in size,
Each planted by her.

So, we gave her some of these trees
Already planted in the ground,
By dropping a seed here and there
She will be having
A Christmas tree
For years to come.

Thank-you for the food.

(Published in "Fly Away," 1997, *Creative with Words Publications*.)

My Vanished Dreams

I built sandcastles of my dreams
With my father on England's
Southern shores.
He was the king, I the princess,
Waiting for my prince
To come one day.

We built sandcastles more
And then the tide came in,
Much further than we had hoped.
Next day, castles and dreams
Had vanished.
I knew then that one day
My father will vanish,
And the prince will not come.

I tossed a stone in defiance
After the endless sea,
Shouting at it
With tears flowing,
Having taken away
Sandcastles and dreams from me.

February 11, 1995

To Become One with Eternity

As I leave the bounds of earth
And soar above the banks of clouds,
A crimson red and golden morning glow
Stretch from the north to the south.
And there between the earth and me
Lie fog and clouds layers deep,
But above all spans an endless blue.
In Goethean Faustian ecstasy
I soar like an eagle, forever free.
And as I travel out into space,
There, in the vastness's embrace,
I lose my earthly self
To become one with eternity.

(Published in "Nature, Vol.2," 1995, *Creative with Words Publications*.)

No Longer Caring

A young man fell off his bike today,
In the middle of an intersection.
Dazed, he picked himself up
And that, which lay scattered by his fall.
Moaning he lifted up his bike.

I, in my car, waited for the light to change,
Hoping the young man will be all right.
Traffic coming the other way,
Circumvented him, and made the turn.
Nonetheless, they and I are afraid,
It could be a fake.

But he moaned.
Was he really hurt?
Only the cold traffic lights
Were in his favor
As he struggled across the street
Past non-caring
Spectators in their cars.

(Published in "Relationships," 1996, *Creative with Words Publications*.)

My Favorite Place

Wherever I hang my hat
Is my favorite place.
It is as easy
As that.

(Published in "An ABC of Favorite Places," 1997, *Creative with Words Publications*.)

I Know Why

I know why autumn
Is the best season of all,
Full of anticipation
Of a festive time to come.

I know why autumn
Is the best season of all.
I remember Mother's warm,
Welcoming light in the window.
I remember her waiting there
Welcoming me home.
I smell the food,
The cookies and the tarts,
Waiting for me along with
A cup of hot chocolate.

I know why autumn
Is the best season of all.
Father takes us hiking
From farm to farm.
From harvest festival
To harvest festival.
Fruit tasting, wine tasting,
Having a ball.

I know why autumn
Is the best season of all.
Memories linger
To warm now my aging heart.

Halfway There

I went to Hawaii, to find Hawaii,
But I did not.
Among tow'ring high-rises
And crowded beaches,
I was lost like a stranger in LA
Or in New York,
No, like a stranger in Miami.
For that, I did not come to Hawaii.

So, I went to the Northshore,
Lodged among pineapple fields.
And there among sugar canes
And sugar mills,
Among smaller homes
And unpretentious people,
An empty beach stretches for miles
With corals from broken up reefs.

I was half-way there.

(Published in "Names," 1996, *Creative with Words Publications*.)

Oh, How to Belong

I saw him riding on his fiery steed,
The best of all in the merry-go-round.
And when I looked again,
The horses were running without a rider.

I saw the parish,
Busily preparing for fiesta,
The master of ceremony at the bandstand,
Knowing all by name, except for mine.

I saw them dancing, young and old,
Children running, riding their bikes,
Chatting and talking, including the police,
But not to me.

I once belonged to a special place
I can't remember when
And why I had ever left it
To venture into a world,
Hostile to all of my beliefs.

I saw . . .
And I was not part of it at all.

(Published in "An ABC of Favorite Places," 1997, *Creative with Words Publications*.)

June 1995

And There I Found It
(Kole Kole Pass)

I stood at the lookout point
High in the mountain range.
Below one mountain tumbling
Gradually into the sea.

Above me execution places
Of once defeated chiefs.
I saw little signs of them today,
Just terraced slopes, stretching,

Bending in the howl of a wind,
Which carries the woes of the past.

And the serenity of a land
Difficult to be described.

As Hawaiian life passed
In front of my searching eyes.
And the roar of the planes
Coming for destruction

One fateful day,
I felt not wanting it
Transposed to a life
I did not know.

And when a calmness befell the pass,
As the western sea calmed,
And in the sky a sun settled
Among the first banks of fog,

Slowly moving in,
I stood in front of God's open book
That revealed human emotions
Of endless proportions.

And before . . .
Before the pages slowly turned
The sun set in the sky
Into a night of a future yet to come.

(Published in "Names," 1996, *Creative with Words Publications*.)

**Waimea Canyon, Kauai;
photo by the author.**

They Did Not Even Ask

I do not even know
Those living behind my yard,

Where I gave Mother Nature
A chance to grow her shrubs and trees.
And when I came home one day.
Without having asked me,
Those living behind my yard
Had cut back my hedge and my tree.

I did not mind that they cut
What was hanging over their side.
But they had cut away
The branches of my tree on my side.

A tree, which a ranger once gave me
And asked me to do
A good deed, helping the town by
Planting a tree.

Tender Caress

The night has kissed
The weary wanderer
With honeysuckle lips
And sent the luring nightingale
To court him in his dreams.

(Published in "Dreams," 1995, *Creative with Words Publications*.)

The Money Tree

I have a dream of a money tree,
Which stands outside just for me.
Oh, my very own money tree,
From which I pick each day some bills
To live a life so free,
Due to this glorious money tree.

Then one day, I awake and what did I see,
There in my yard a money tree,
My money tree with bills and coins
Just standing there for me.
I rush outside to a carefree life,
To pick the money, crisp and ripe,
But when I got there, what could it be,
What lies there in front of the money tree?

There was a note from the government,
"If you pick a penny from this tree,
Half of that penny belongs to me.
So think before you claim this tree
Your very own to be."

And when I looked again, I saw
The tree vanishing from my sight.
Sadly I turned
And walked back inside.

(Published in "Dreams," 1995, *Creative with Words Publications*.)

Running Through the Blooming Meadows

My mother died when I was very young,
And ever since she tries to take me along,
Running with her
Through the blooming meadows.

I was my father's one and all.
He guarded me with doctors
From that fate.

One day, out in a foreign land
Where all thought that I was safe,
My father with doctors spent
To get advice how with medication,
I should be on the mend.

That day, alone out on the ranch
My guardian tended to his stock.
I went to him, I needed him,
My mother's perfume filled the air.
I fell into my guardian's arms
And silently passed away.

Now, I'm running through the blooming meadows
With my mother by my side,
While at my freshly dug up grave
My father stands and silently he cries.

What Is a Ball?

It might be a pearl to a mermaid,
A pebble of worth to those who seek.
It might be a leather firmness
To those who like to play.
It might be a spot of dirt
To scarabs rolling it along.
It might be the sun
To those who seek its warmth.
It might be a bit of dust
Space stuff needs to form.
It might be a piece of ice
Comets drag behind.

It might be the earth itself
To all who live upon her.
What is a ball?
It might be a pearl to a mermaid.

(Published in one of the Carmel, California, publications.)

The Second Generation

It is not until you have left your home,
Young in age, not knowing,
Following your parents to other shores
That you feel the pain of a loss.

A loss you cannot describe
And cannot explain to anyone,
Because no one understands.

You have been born in one land,
Stuck it out with parents in another,
Being at home in neither,
And you are burdened
With always being the outsider.

Had it not been for the book with words
Of the language so familiar to you.
The only hold of something you had,
Which has been taken away from you.

How could you have made it all these years
And still had all the hurt you cannot explain,
Because no one seems to understands?

(The author's sudden memory returned of having had to leave her adopted country where she felt at home.)

There's Feasting at that House

It's just an old dog's water bowl,
An old cat's feeding dish,
But everyday there's leftover
From the indoor cats
And humans,
And so we come.

There's feasting at that house
For all the strays,
The lame old dog,
The opossum three,
The family raccoon
Of four or five or six,
One without a tail,
The other lame,
And all the birds
That come to stay
In Spring and Fall,
And all those,
Frightened by a storm.

There's feasting at that house
For one and all,
And so we come.

(Submitted to *The Carmel Valley Sun*, September 4, 1995.)

Look for Me

Shall I not return, look for me
By the Buddha in his peaceful tree.
You might not find me there
Because it's merely my soul lingering
Among chirping birds and warming sun.
In the smallest little eco-system
Right here in the midst of LA town,
Where butterflies and birds meet,
At night the rabbits and the deer,
And next to me the one who knows,
"Fluttering Wings" in Indian lore.

Shall I not return from there
Don't shed a tear.
Around me are trees with lives to spare
A thousand life times more,
I could ever think to live,
And thousand times of nature's lives
Is so much more than any man can have.

So, shall I not return, look for me
By the Buddha in his peaceful tree.

(Reminiscent of a visit to the Buddha with a friend of the author.)

When Is Scorning Right?

Can it ever be
That scorning may be right?
Yes, it can when the bull
Moved into the horses' ranch.
The bull convinced to be a horse.
The horses convinced he is a bull.

Their minds were set
They did not meet.
A shuffling of hoofs,
A kicking of dust,
A neighing into the air
Told everyone otherwise.

Today, the bull enjoys his life
With goats and pot-bellied pigs.
And, of course, with the duck,
Who thinks
She is a pig . . .

A Rose in Friendship

I know if you wanted a rose,
It had to have a scent,
But a long-stemmed rose
Hardly ever gives a scent.
For that, I need to give you a rose
From my English garden, growing wild,
Where in all shades roses grow
With aromas so tantalizing wild.

Then if a rose is always a rose
That bears harming thorns,
I'll take shears to the rose
And trim off all its thorns.
No harm will come from that rose,
But I will show to you
With that scented, thornless rose,
How true a friend I will be to you.

(Based on a gift by the author to her friend.)

There Is a Light

There is a light
They're shining it on me,
Letting the performer know
Who I might be.

Crossing the Stream

You showed me the way
How to cross the wide stream.
So I did it,
And swam across.
I did it again,
Dodging the waves
Of boats and ships.
And on the last crossing
I took you with me.
You swam up to a point
So, I carried you across
The rest of the way.

(Published in the August 1998 edition of *the Eclectics!*)

Where Did My Flag Go?

It was there just yesterday
As the bugler blew Reveille.
I stopped the car in reverence.
Today, the bugler bugled
And I stopped.
But the flag was no longer there.

I was wondering what to salute:
An empty flagpole,
The dirt around it,
Dug up in anticipation,
As rumors go, for three slabs
Of the wall that once
Divided East and West
Of Berlin?
In the meantime, I am
In search of my flag.

Somebody told me
It has been moved
To the soldiers' cemetery.
Temporarily, I hope!

Joy to the Flag

Joy to you, flag,
So battle-worn and torn,
Dug from rubbles
You survived,
To be honored again
And again,
And again . . .

September 4, 1995

Bagel Bakery

I rush at lunchtime
From here to there
To everywhere,
To do my shopping anywhere.
Pick up the mail,
Sneak in a doctor's visit,
But I declare,
I do not miss my favorite shop,
For bagel pizza, bagel dog,
For bagel sticks,
Or even a sandwich mix,
With a friend or more,
Discussing a work–related chore.
I only wish there would be
Close to work a bagel bakery.

(Published in "Travels Through Time," 1997, *Creative with Words Publications*.)

Island Visit
(Reminiscing a visit to Catalina Island.)

I came to the island on a hot summer day,
Beaches were crowded, cruise ships everywhere.
Tour boat travelers had come in full score.
There was little for me to do on shore.

I sat and guessed who the locals were
Who mostly stayed behind closed doors.
The cruise ships sailed away, tour boats pulled out.
Left was the island and me.

I could walk its streets, hike through its hills,
Take in the spectacular sights it offered still.

When it was time for me to go
In the shimmer of a late afternoon sun's glow,
From harbor waves I could only see
The island people, their homes, their hills,
Not to go, they were begging me . . .

Enveloped in fog, the island soon was moving away,
Then it had disappeared from my view.
The mainland was not yet in sight,
Left were rolling waves, a tossing sea, to my left and right.
And I stood on deck, I was truly sad,
Holding back farewell tears.

(Published in "Travel: Going Places," 1998, *Creative with Words Publications*.)

Somewhere Out There

Somewhere out there
Where the day's dying sun
Meets the toss of the relentless sea,
That is where I want to be.

Somewhere out there
Where tossing errant winds
Cool all my ills,
Where restless waves and calling gulls
Heal all my ails.

(Published in "Travel: Going Places," 1998, *Creative with Words Publications*.)

One Way or the Other

When I look out of the window
The ocean seems to shrink,
Smaller is my view.
Growing tall and wide
Around me are luscious shrubs.
Do I have the heart
Cutting back the foliage
To enjoy a broader view
Of the wide ocean
Once lying there
In front of me?

(Published in "Nature . . ." 1998, *Creative with Words Publications*.)

San Diego

It once was . . .
Now, what did they say
About a one-horse town?
It was a bit larger,
But by not much more.
Forty years have passed,
I have been to Moscow,
To Paris, to Munich,
Panama City, Honolulu,
Toronto, Los Angeles,
San Francisco, to name a few.

It's still a one-horse town
In comparison to those . . .
But what a jewel it is
Lying there by the sea,
San Diego!

(Published in "Travel: Going Places," 1998, *Creative with Words Publications*.)

Las Vegas, Today—Tomorrow!

What is Las Vegas?
A paradise one could say
With a whiff of danger indeed
As it is today.

Tomorrow, maybe
Ten-thousand years from now,
Archaeologists will look at the town,
"What does this mean?" they'll ponder.
"It must be a religious symbol,
Of some sort,"
They conclude, as they still wonder.

(Published in the December 1999 edition of *the Eclectics!*)

My Best Friend

When I hear a raven's call,
To the window I rush with glee,
To see if he comes at all
To the branch near to me.

I have the patience,
More than Job ever had,
And sit and wait
And wait and sit.

And when he comes
To the branch near to me
I tremble all over for joy.
The raven cocks its head and caws,
"Silly, chum, I'm a stately bird
And you are a mere cat.

The crow that comes daily to
the author's house apparently to
protect it; photo by the author.

~ 114 ~

We can't be friends.
Nature made no allowance for that."

"Phooey to nature," I declare.
"I love your call, and when you do
To the window I rush,
Waiting for you."

(Published in "Animals, Loving & Caring," 1999, *Creative with Words Publications*.)

Workplace Turned into a Zoo

Have you ever heard
A workplace
Turning into a zoo?
Well, it's true.
Mine is a zoo.
And not due to the
Doings of those
Dropped off cats and
Dogs abandoned there.
But the wide open space
The lawns and
Freshly cut grass
Attract the deer,
The fox, the raccoon,
The opossum.
En mass.

Have You Ever . . .
(A later version.)

Have you ever heard a workplace
Turning into a zoo?
Well, it's true. Mine is,
And not due to doings of those
Abandoned cats and dogs.
Sloping hills of grass and woods,
Freshly cut lawns and
Succulent grasses,
Invite deer to freely roam,
Protected from danger.
And on their way north
Canada geese have
Made it their home as well.
Silently, the deer graze,
And loudly honk the geese
Snatching up goodies
From among slender hoofs.

(Inspired by a Texas fort. Published in the "Animals, Loving & Caring," 1999, *Creative With Words Publications.)*

The Stranger

As I stepped out of the woods,
Leaving ski lifts and slopes behind,
I stepped onto a freshly harvested field,
Where stubs of cut-down wheat
Clutch themselves as they break off
Onto my clothes.

Far ahead of me, miniature in size,
I see a reaper woman
Once again harvesting fields already cleared,
And as I approach her
She and I grow comparably in size.
She quickly covers her basket with a cloth
And hurries back to town,
Which spills down a mountain side.

She did not know
That I too had been afraid of strangers.
And thus, I had walked tall and proud
To let her know
One just does not mess with me.

(Reminiscent of a stroll from Sandberg to Schloßberg, Bopfingen, Germany; published in "Holidays! With a Whisper of Seasons!" 1998, *Creative with Words Publications*.)

Discarded Humans

I can't believe that here I sit
Applying for unemployment.
Yet able and willing to work,
Denied by those I am working for.
For forty-one years I have worked,
Appreciated by those
Who gave me a job,
Knowing that I give my all.
And I gave my all . . .
Now, I am discarded, claimed useless,
And determined nonessential,
As I apply for unemployment.

(Published in the November 23, 1995, edition of *The Carmel Valley Sun*, during a furlough from work.)

At the Edge of Forever

As I stand at the edge of forever,
The stars guide me on a journey
Beyond all time barriers,
Allowing me a glimpse of the essence
Of all things that were and are
And forever will be.

(Published in the March 1998 edition of *the Eclectics!*)

Nile Beauty

There's a ship waiting at the Nile banks
To let me know, it sends out a call.
It is time to leave the sites of the ancients,
The vendors in their multi-colored stalls.

There's a ship stranded on a sandbank,
Others shine their searching lights so bright
To aid a fellow Nile traveler
To bring its cargo to deeper channel site.

There's a ship floating down the river,
Passing banks with a life standing still
For those trying to make a living,
As ancestors did a thousand years since.

There are carriages drawn by horses
Along the banks of the River Nile.
There are water taxis churning
To take passengers to spectacular sites.

There's a ship anchored at the Nile bank
Waiting for passengers anew.
And I turn to cast a thankful nod
To bid the ship and water way adieu.

(Inspired by a cruise taken by the author down the River Nile in Egypt at Christmas time. Published in "Names,"
1996, *Creative with Words Publications*.)

R. C. Gorman

I sat among old adobes,
Inspired by an art gallery
Across the patio,
Sensing beauty in serenity.

I searched for the maiden
With the chili basket at her side.
She wasn't to be found
Much like other treasures
I searched for in my life.

R. C. Gorman,
Where are you hiding her?

(Published in "Names," 1996, *Creative with Words Publications.*)

The Kiss

I kissed my horse
And he kissed me back,
Nudged my face,
Gave me a shove.
Love was not what lacked.

I awoke next morning
Not battered or bruised,
But full of poison oak
On every spot where my
Horse had smooched.

(Published in "Humor," 1996, *Creative with Words Publications.*)

The Bed of Moss

I slept upon a bed
So silken soft,
Warmed by the setting
Summer's sun.

I dreamt of riches
Incomparably
To things the world
Can give.

I woke upon a
Gentle kiss
Of summer's
Rising sun,

And stirred from my
Mossy bed
Embracing riches
Only nature bears.

(Published in "Nature, Vol. 5," 1995, *Creative with Words Publications.*)

Monterey, California, USA

1996

February 17, 1996

Last Night I Lost My Dog

Last night I dreamed, I lost my dog.
I had no idea where and when.
But when I came home, he was not there.
I searched the places, I had gone with him,
To find him not anywhere
Waiting for me.
And when I awoke from this dream
To my relief, he was there
In the room with the cats,
Wagging his tail, licking tears from my face.

And then I truly opened my eyes,
Only to realize
All had just been a dream.
And my dog had died
More than three years ago.

**Sundance, the author's pet;
photo by the author.**

(Published in "In the Love of Animals," 1996, *Creative with Words Publications.*)

A Redwings' Birth

Unexpectedly,
At least not yet,
One morning in the stable
Of the Mustang mare
There was a second head,
Peeking eyes at the outsider.
Four perfect legs, equipped
With hoofs, a fluffy tail—
A little foal had arrived.
"It is a boy."

Tired from the ordeal of birth,
You lay on a pile of hay
While mother stood watch.
After occasional trips to
The milk source, your legs
Grew strong, your ears flicked.
You were alert, trying to take
A few running steps,
Uncoordinated at first,
Toward Mother, even a
Hesitating step toward us,
The proud aunts and uncles,
Grandparents, sisters, and brothers.
Whatever you might want to call
Us, only to find safety,
Warmth, and caring
Next to your ever-present mother.
"Welcome, little fellow."

(Inspired by the birth of Mirage on the horse sanctuary, Redwings, April 20, 1996.)

Monterey, California, USA

1997

No specific date other than 1997

Insect Attack!

Why is it that
Whenever I go
Into the vast outdoors,
Insects swarm around me
From far and near,
To take a bite out of me?

Yet, my spouse
Can go anywhere,
Day and night,
Coming back without
A single insect bite!

(Published in "In the Company of Animals," 1997, *Creative with Words Publication*.)

Mother Quail

Let me tell you a tale.
One day,
My eight-year-old and I went to the fair.
After seeing all of this
And all of that,
And all of everything,
Both of us needed a rest.

And as we sat on the grass,
Son few feet ahead of me,
From nowhere a mother quail
And her brood appeared.
Bypassing me, safe in space,
She left her little ones
With my son.

And off she went to have
Some adult quail fun.
My eight-year-old
Looking up at me
With great surprise
In his deep brown eyes.

Moments later then
Mother quail returned,
Picked up her brood
And off they went.

(Published in "In the Company of Animals," 1997, *Creative with Words Publications*.)

Mr. Woodpecker

Mr. Woodpecker, what did you do?
You pecked a hole in my tree.
You left a mess each day you pecked,
A mess of wood chips for me to clear.

As day and night pass their hands,
I hear your chirp as you come
Cautiously approaching your new home,
And then you silently slip in.

Mr. Woodpecker, am I supposed
To be honored by your choice.
Or do I have to call the tree surgeon
To encourage your moving on?

(Published in "In the Company of Animals," 1997, *Creative with Words Publications*.)

Sports Widow

She followed him from town to town,
Wherever he played.
She sat, his only spectator,
On rain-soaked bleachers,
Her red umbrella shielding her.
She shivered in icy-cold days,
Her feet frozen in the snow
Even though she wore boots.
She went to his practice,
She went to his plays,
She went to his parties,
She went with him everywhere.
Her only friends, his friends,
Sports buddies all the way.
She did this not to become
Like her friends, a forgotten
Sports widow waiting at home.

(Reminiscent of the author accompanying her play-by-play broadcaster husband. Published in "Sports, Hobbies, Talents," 1997, *Creative with Words Publications*.)

Junior

Junior, now that was a horse.
A Percheron with four sturdy legs,
A gray mane and a swooshy tail,
A sturdy body.
He was a beautiful gray
Which turned to silvery stars.

I cannot say more.
And when I stood
Next to him,
He hung his head
And went to sleep.
My first thoughts were

Am I boring him?
But then I realized,
He felt as comfortably
With me standing there
As I did with him
Nodding next to me.

I love you, Junior.

Junior; photo by the author.

Monterey, California, USA

1998

No specific date other than 1998

Status of Senior Citizens

Fifty and something,
Fifty AND something.
Decrepit old lady
Teaches computer programing?
Young buck at the computer store
Flips out!

(Published in "Humor," 1998, *Creative with Words Publications*.)

High Meadows

She was very little when we took her
On her first outing, Sabina, the boxer girl.
Eight weeks? Maybe ten? But not more.
She loved the outdoors, the
Coolness of Arizona high meadows.
It was the first time, I saw her standing
Looking back at me.
"Are you coming to play with me?"
Her eyes seemed to ask.

The second time, I saw her standing
In the park, looking back at me,
"I'm so sorry," she said, "I can't anymore."
The next day, Sabina passed away.

In memory of the author's boxer dog, Sabina; published in "Nature . . . " 1998, *Creative with Words Publications*; photo taken with the author's camera of her and of Sabina; possibly by son Spencer wo is a fine photographer himself.

Whispers of Festivities

The crispness of air
That brushed against my face
Early this morning,
Rode upon the wings
Of autumn's first rains.

Touches of crackling fires,
And ripeness in the fields
Filled the air with whispers
Of festivities to come.

(Published in the March 1998 edition of *the Eclectics!*)

June 5, 1998

Our Friends of the Past

I can't believe the many farewells we had to say.
Our friends of the past are gone.
Pictures and memories remind us
Of the love they gave, the company they were,
The fun together we shared.

There are the dogs: the shepherd, the boxer,
The good, good, old black Lab . . .
There are the strays: Blue—the faithful tom;
Old Man—the one with the busiest schedule in town,
Making the rounds from place to place;

Feisty—feisty Jenna—the lady cat with attitude;
But the sweetest of them all,
The half-lame dog of no name,
The blind mother raccoon . . .
There are the cats, pets they were,
Tippy, the wise age-old sage;
Bunny, the Calico, just wanting to be with us.
They are all gone now.
Years have passed and yet,
My heart still aches for every one of them.

(Published in "In the Company of Animals," 1997, *Creative with Words Publications*.)

My Fair Daughter

Good old Henry Higgins
Married Eliza, the sweet.
They had one child together,
A little girl indeed.
Then Eliza fell ill
And died a sudden death,
Leaving Henry Higgins
To raise his daughter at his best.
He finally had his chance
To form her to be like him.
But what do you think did happen?
The little girl turned out to be
More like her departed mother
To poor Henry Higgins' chagrin.

A Ghost Town While Living

I went home one day
To the place where I was born.

It had been eighty years or so,
The town was almost gone.
And what remained
Were shambles and ruins,
Grave markers broken and thrown,
No one there . . .

I stood alone among trees and grass,
Memories came of long time ago.
People busied themselves in this town
With daily chores.
Now, they are gone.
Nature has taken over the place
To be the same as back in time
Before this town made it on the map,
And my ancestors had come
To give my family life . . .

(Published in the June 1999 edition of *the Eclectics!*)

Memories

You carried within you memories
Such jubilant days
Of celebrating holidays
Down on the farm.
Now you are gone,
And I carry the memories
Of holidays I shared with you.

But when I am gone,
Who will share the memories
With those coming after me,
Having never been
Down on the farm?

View from Outer Space

As I sit here in outer space
And look down at Earth,
The Northern Lights span the globe
After the flames of a setting sun.
Down on Earth a day is done.

But up here in space
Around and around I go,
Enjoying every moment
I see the globe,
Which tells me somewhere
Down there
Is the home to which I belong.

Shopping Observation

I had to do a last-minute shopping.
Promised the spouse to do just that.
Had twenty minutes time
Before the spouse would come to pick me up.
A bench was there for the weary, elderly shopper,
Right by the express checkout.
Not that I was weary or elderly,
But my spouse was never on time.

I saw the strangest combinations checked through:
A pound of butter with milk and some eggs,
Certainly forgotten items from the weekly buy.
Then there was the one with nine bottles of wine,
A party perhaps, a weekend's delight?
How about the one with the frozen dinner
And pre-prepared dessert.

Obviously a bachelor.
And then, well, he had two bottles of water,
Two mushrooms, and one banana.
His purchase was not clear for sure.
The strangest of them all
Was the lady with a bag of kitty litter
And a roll of film!

(Published in the August 1998 edition of *the Eclectics!*)

Monterey, California, USA

(The author along with her friends were wondering whether life on Earth would continue at the turn of the century. The computers did not seem to promise that. It was getting close to the year 2000.)

1999

No specific date other than 1999

Will There Be a Tomorrow?

What will we do
If the Earth comes to a halt
And there will be
No tomorrow
Beyond the last day
Of the year?
What will we do?

Did You Know . . .

Did you know Santa and Mrs. Claus
Do not live at the North Pole?
They live in Carmel, maybe in Carmel Valley.
Just somewhere in Carmel, yes indeed!

The first time I saw them was Boxing Day last year.
Both were recuperating from delivering all over the world.
They had a leisure breakfast,
She in her red jacket and blue cap,
He in his nicely groomed beard.

She ate a hearty dish of eggs and hash browns,
He drank coffee as he scanned the papers on Boxing Day.

The next time I saw them was after Halloween this year.
Both were shopping for Christmas cookies and candies,
Even for a cheese log here and there.
He was well-groomed in his white beard,
She wore her red jacket and blue cap.

They readied themselves to go to the North Pole
To help loading the toys, giving their hard-working elves
The cookies and candies and logs of cheese,
Which they had purchased in Carmel.

(Published in "Nature / Seasons," 1999, *Creative with Words Publications*.)

Who's to Blame?

Summer time!
Heat, sun, no rain!
Havoc everywhere.
Deer rush into suburbs
In search of water bowls
Left by domesticated
Cats and dogs,
Nibbling buds of Nile Lilies.
Raccoons scramble
For water and shelter
From the heat.

Sorry.

Damage everywhere!
But who can blame them?
They have equal rights to
Nature's warehouse of goods.
Only mankind, with his needs,
Interferes.

(Published in "Animals," 1999, *Creative with Words Publications*.)

At Times, Friends Part

There was a heart-rending farewell
At the piers where ships
Wait in New York harbor to sail for
Southampton, England.
    A rich little English girl, who had come
    For treatment against Polio,
    Had befriended one of the
    Horse-drawn carriage drivers
    And his horse, outside the Plaza.

    They stood on the pier,
    The horse neighing,
    The man with hat in hand,
    "Good-bye little English princess,"
    He said, as she gave him a hug
    And cuddled the horse.
    On the arms of her father
    Going up the gang plank,
    She waved and sent tiny kisses of love
    To the carriage driver and the horse.

So the newspapers reported sometime
In the beginning of the nineteen hundreds.

(Published in "2000 Love 0002," 1999, *Creative with Words Publications*.)

Back Home

Heaven is truly the place
Where you felt most comfortable while alive.
I went back to my home in Africa,
To Kalua Estates outside of Kitale,
In the Trans Nzoia District,
To a working farm,
And there I sensed the spirits
Of my father and mother
And the sibling, who was never meant to be.
It was a comfortable feeling,
But one which made me sad.
They were at a place they loved most
In life and I was still here
Rather of necessity in a place,
Not of desire,
Not of comfortable feeling . . .

As I left Kalua and those who loved it so
I could not help but shed a tear, wondering,
Was it just a dream, a hope . . .
Or more?

(Published in "2000 Love 0002," 1999, *Creative with Words Publications*.)

Could That Be Love?

He, a financier of a prestigious firm,
Tall, dark, well-groomed and mannered,
Suits tailored, eligible.

She, a free spirit, traipsing the world,
Loose jeans and Ts, hair pigtailed,
Vagrant looks everywhere, eligible.

They met in his office,
He advising her to invest in futures,
Just as her father had said.

Years later, he traipsed the world
In search of something, somewhere.
Still tall, gray hair longer, jeans and Ts.

She, now an office manager,
Hair coiffed, clothes measured to fit.
Shoes elegantly styled
And polished to a sheen.

They met at a flea market,
He peddling souvenirs of his trips,
She looking for that rare antique . . .

(Published in "2000 Love 0002," 1999, *Creative with Words Publications*.)

Evening Embrace

It seems as if the evening sky
With golden arms
Tucked the earth to sleep,
Gently kissing it goodnight.

Stretch-Limo Ride

I won a stretch-limo ride,
For me and my bride.
What thrill to be picked up,
Escorted by hotel management,
Photographs taken everywhere.
I learned the royal wave
To everyone around.

Even to those inside the café.
And then we were off
Behind pulled-down dark shades.
I kissed my bride and embraced
The luxury I suddenly
Seemed to have found.

No Challenge

If I could see everything of life,
If I could hear everything of life,
If I could feel everything of life,
If I could taste everything of life,
What would life be?

There would be no challenge.

(Published in the January 2006 edition of *the Eclectics!*)

High Desert Sunset

A sky steel blue
Separated from
Orange sunset
By a layer of
Fluffy dark clouds,
Fringed with rainy
Streaks like the
Unravelling hem
Of a linen skirt.
Below a city flickers
Thousand fold
Its lights in a
Still warm desert air:
High desert sunset.

**Streaks of sunset;
photo by the author.**

(Published in "Elements," 1997, *Creative with Words Publications*.)

The Germanic Sun

When I was a little one, five or four or three,
I knew on whose side I wanted to be.
"The sun," I proclaimed. "Is my mother.
She kindly tends to me like none other,
And when I'm especially good,
She serves me pancakes as sustaining food."

(Published in "Space: The Sky—The Heavens," 1997, *Creative with Words Publications*.)

Tropical Twilight

It has dwindled to a few moments
This day of reassurance of life.
The sun can no longer have it.
In a last grasp it sets down,
Drawing circles of red and gold,
Afloat on a thousand-wave sea,
All to dissipate in the darkness of night
As it seizes land and water.
And mountains melt with the heavens
Into a depthless darkening sky
From where the peacock shrills,
And a hyena laughs.
I blow out the lamp,
Which had cast my shadow
On the wall of my tent.

Sunset on one of the author's cruise evenings, photo by the author.

Two Double Tercet Reversed

Waves
Splashing
High up shores,
Falling down
Ebbing
Off.

A
Star born,
Shines and lives,
Burning out,
Falling
Gone.

(Both published in the *SPAFASWAP*.)

Idle Not Your Love

I saw her, an elderly woman,
Having in common with me
Tending to her lawn
And sweeping cut grass.
And my mother—
Thousands of miles away—
Does the same.

I wanted to call her, *Mother*.
For within me I carry love,
And for my mother—
Thousands of miles away—
Someone might do the same.

I saw her, an elderly woman,
Having in common with me,
Being alone
And a loved one
Thousands of miles away.

(Revised version of "In Common with Me" in *Stepping through Time*. "Idle Not Your Love" was published in the May 1976 edition of *The Creative with Words Club*.)

June 1999

Spring 1999

At a time when things are
No longer right
In far off lands,
Trees don their
Branches in thousands
Of dainty blossoms
Emitting scents
Of tranquil sweetness.

(Published in the June 1999 edition of *the Eclectics!*)

August 1999

Earth and Heaven, Fog and Dew

Mother Earth and Father Heaven
Once were one in total darkness.
There was no light.
Their sons tried to separate them,
All but one succeeded.
Wind refused.
Out of the separation grew light
And with light mankind saw itself,
And with sight came realization,
Mankind could be free.

It was sad to see Mother Earth
Yearning for Father Heaven.
Her tears, as fog rose up to heaven.
His tears, as dew fell down to earth.
Wind took to the heavens
To be with his father and to
Avenge his brothers for all times.

(Published in the August 1999 edition of *the Eclectics!*)

From the Rockies to the Sea

Every now and then
You pick a vacation
When the weather is with you
All the way.

This has been such a vacation.
St. Peter had been kind.
The sun was shining every day.
Only when we left the Rockies
Did the heavens open up
And cry, just a little though.
Not much, and only overnight.

And when we were out at sea,
I have never seen such calmness,
Just millions and millions of waves,
None of them capped with white foam.

There was no sorrow anywhere.
Poseidon was at peace
With his daughters.
And the angels in the heavens
Above had no clouds from where
To do their tiny pranks,
Annoying the traveler.

(Published in the December 1999 edition of *the Eclectics!*)

Monterey, California, USA

(And Earth continued in its turns after January 1. There was no problem. The computers did just fine. The author's sister, Ursula Ingrid Kristensen, née Geldreich, passed away October 2, 2001.)

2000—2001

No specific date other than 2001

The author's sister, Ursula Ingrid Kristensen, née Geldreich; photo by Ursula's in-laws in Denmark

Let Me Embrace You

Let me embrace you.
Most of the nineteen hundreds
I have been with you.
It was all of my life
And you almost all of your
Existence.
You are all I know.
Let me embrace you.

Let me embrace you.
The two thousands

Had you one day slip away,
It was October 2nd.
You are forever gone.
And with you my
Familiarity.
All what I know
Is gone with you.
Let me embrace you . . .
One more time—

(Upon the passing of the author's sister, October 2, 2001.)

Monterey, California, USA

(The author started to travel throughout the United States in order to train teachers and U.S. military in computer usage in language teaching/learning. This meant several trips to Hawaii.)

2002

March 16, 2002

Oahu!

Every time I leave Oahu,
There is that moisture in the air.
Is it just a fond farewell
Or a parting hard to bear?

Last time when I left Oahu,
The skies had cried a heavy tear.
This time it was a little sprinkle,
"You are to us so very dear."

Next time I come to Oahu,
For a while I will stay.
There will be smiles around me.
Wiping tears away.

I Cry Each Day a Little Less

I cried when my father passed away.
He was ill, very ill.
Soon I was happy for him to have passed.
I cried when my mother passed away.
She did not know herself
What was the matter with her.
Alzheimer had ruffed her away.

Then my sister passed away
For no worldly reason whatsoever.
I cannot stop crying.
A part of me has gone,
I cannot find it,
No matter where I look,
Being so incomplete,
Missing her. And I cry,
I cry each day a little less.
I know
Time will eventually
Heal this pain as well.

From left: the author and her big sister, Ursula; photo by the author's mother.

April 20, 2002

A Sister's Opinion

"I am the golden child,"
My sister used to stress,
Wearing golden jewelry.
"You are the silver child."

I like silver.
There was nothing wrong with that.

Today, my sister is gone
And I have her golden jewelry,
And wear it along
With my silvery baubles.

They go
Well together.

When I was Young

I was busy
When young.
As a child
I knitted,
I crocheted
Baby outfits
For the ladies
At the Old
Folks home.

As reward
I always received
A small dish,
A glassy container
For butter or jam,
And much more.

I still have
All of them
Today.

(Reminiscent of the author's childhood.)

Glass jar received by author for knitting
baby booties; photo by the author.

Backstage Flutter

Lines are forming,
Relatives and friends are waiting,
Bearing flowers, cameras poised,
Backstage hearts are aflutter,
Stomachs ache.
The curtain rises,
Musicians play,
And they dance.
Ballerinas of all ages
Float over the stage.
The roar of the crowd,
Flashlights illuminate,
Gone are all worries
Until . . .
Until next time.

(Published in the July 2002 edition of *the Eclectics!*)

Song of the Past

I listened to a song of the past,
Where a little pub at the corner
Is a place where nobody cares
What you have and who you are.

I listened to a song of the past,
Where the food is just a sandwich,
And the bill is on the coaster,

You or everyone else has credit.

I listened to a song of the past,
Where everyone knew each other
And everyone cared,
Where love and trust were true.

I listened to a song of the past,
And wondered what has happened
In the years gone by
To make us what we are today.

I listened to a song of the past
. . .

(Submitted to the August edition of *The Monterey County Post*.)

September 2002

The Pageant of Fall

A gentle breeze,
At first it seemed,
Caressed the world
In summer glow,
But then a crested ocean
Tossed its waves
On rocky shores
And brought along
A wind that blew
A crisper air
Across the land.

Trees, decked in
Shimm'ring gold

Send quiv'ring leaves
In kaleidoscopic fall
To colder grounds.
The pageant has begun
Where nature goes to rest
In dreams of million
Leaves and blooms
When gentle breezes
Once again
Ride on calmer seas.

(Submitted to the annual *Poetry Shell* of the Monterey
Peninsula poetry contest.)

A Priori

Within ourselves
We hold myriads of universes—
Each more intricate
Than the other,
Each more complex—
All holding in themselves
The sum total of
Knowledge,
Of all there is.
If only we could
Tab this resource.

Pros and Cons

"Aligator Warning" the sign said plainly and clearly.
And I of alligator and crocodile fear
Trudged through the tall grass
And over the water on a stretched-out path
In search of this most fearsome beast.

"Is there a death wish in me," I had to ask.
"That I would take on such a dangerous task?"
With the first rustle, the first snap of a weed,
I rush home to my room and to my bed
To escape this fearsome beast.

(Published in "Animals," 2002, *Creative with Words Publications.*)

Fog

High walls of gray and white fog
Cover what lies below and beyond.
To the newcomer, it is a mystery.
Is there a valley, are there fields?
Then the sun pierces the wall,
Gently at first, a beam at a time,
Then in full force.
The fog lifts and disappears.
Below lies a gentle bay,
And beyond it rise mountains high,
Stretching all the way from earth to the sky.

(Rewrite of "What Lies Beyond?")

What Lies Beyond?

High walls of dark and white fog
Cover what lies below and beyond.
To the newcomer it is a mystery.
Is there a valley? Are there fields?
Then the sun pierces the wall,
Gently at first, a beam at a time,
Then in full force.
The fog lifts and . . .

Below lies a gentle bay
And beyond stretch mountains
As far as the eye can see.

(Published in the August 1999 edition of *the Eclectics!*)

Oblivion

Sometimes when I drive and feel most agitated
I want my car to sprout wings
And fly off into the vast oblivion.

I want my car to take me where there is peace
And love and quiet all around,
And where everyone understands each other.

No matter how hard I try to urge on my car,
It does not sprout desired wings.
I find myself on this earth and a tear falls.

(Published in "A Collection of 2002 Themes!" 2002, *Creative with Words Publications.*)

Mungo

I once knew a dog,
Mungo was his name.
He was neither shepherd
Nor wolf, but was the same.
Mother was Senta,
The gentle shepherd,
Father a wolf back in those
Polish hinterlands.

Mungo was wild,
The protector of the land,
But his soul was mild,
So very kind I knew it
When climbing into his hut.

Telling him what made me happy,
Telling him what made me sad,
Mungo always listened.
And we sat and we sat,
I tightly hugging him,
He gently licking my face.

**Mungo on chain, his mother
Senta in the front; photo
by Martchen Lohse.**

(Reminiscent of a dog the author knew in Ostrada, Poland.)

Pelicans Flying South

Flying high, seagulls sending them off.
The day is crisp and cold,
Fishing no longer is an option
Along the northern shores.
Sunshine and warm water beg,
And once again the arrow

Of pelicans points south,
Pelicans are flying there.
It's a forecast, winter is close.
So are harsh times.

The Bridal Waterfall

As the water tumbles
Down the mountain side,
Each drop has its moment
Of joy and delight.
Forming with thousands
Of other drops it does
A spectacular game.
And the spirit in the water
Is always the same.
Attired in bridal gown,
And in thousand-fold lace,
A waterfall tumbles down.

(Published in "Nature, Vol. 3," 1995, *Creative with Words Publications*.)

Waterfall near Bergen, Norway; photo by the author.

I Am Still the Sea

You might be the gulls
That hover and dive
For food that is near,
At my water's spray,
You probe the essence of me.
I am the sea.

You might be the fish
That silently swims my depths
In schools and pacts
And often quite alone,
As you move restlessly.
I am the sea.

You might be the sailor

Who sets out to master me.
You cross my tossing waves
In search of fish and distant shore.
You try to conquer me.
I am the sea.

You ram your ships,
Oh, sailor man, and fight your kind
On crested waves, I toss you back
From where you came.
You might believe to conquer me,
But I am still the sea.

(Published in "Nature, Vol. 3," 1995, *Creative with Words Publications.*)

Howhowi (Jojoba)

Your home the arid rocky soil
Where desolate Mexican lands merge
With those of the USA,
Your hardiness will outlive
The king of the desert.

Cotton needs water and power,
You can live with little of both.
Your roots tap the water table
To thirty-five feet below.

**Jojoba nut; photo
from the Internet.**

You will be the major crop
For a time to come.
The yields of your fruit are numerous,
Nuts to chew and oil as liquid gold.

As truly as unique liquid wax,
Nuts for coffee-like drinks,
Medicine purposes galore,
You even control erosion of soil.

No wonder, bumper stickers
Proudly proclaim to all,
"I am a jojoba nut!"
The hope of survival of the desert
With multitudes of
Industrial applications.

(Published in "Nature, Vol. 4," 1995, *Creative with Words Publications*.)

Golden Day

Golden is the morning sky
As rain is on its way,
Golden are the rings that
Keep my lover close.

Golden is the hair
Of my only child,
Golden is the wedding ring
Of Grandma long passed on.

Golden is the color of my cat,
A heaven-sent friendly guest.
Golden are the years I now approach.
Golden is my deepest hope.

Long Forgotten

The long forgotten call
Of the mourning dove,
Wooing its mate.
The long forgotten friendly talk.

Greetings are for you everywhere
The long forgotten food,
Filling your hunger and more
To make you live.
These are sites you remember with
As we travel to the home of my past.
The long forgotten desert home
Offering shelter to those living within.

The long forgotten scent of orange blossoms,
Shading passage ways everywhere.
The long forgotten desert folk,
Teaching us their way of life.

The long forgotten cultural friends,
All having moved away.
The long forgotten eternal sun
Burning now the desert land.

The long forgotten sycamore and saguaro
Blooming brightly in spring.
The long forgotten whine of the train,
Which pulls through
Towns so many times.

The long-forgotten . . .

The Long Forgotten

The long forgotten call
Of the mourning dove
Wooing, courting its mate.
The long forgotten friendly folk.
Greeting one everywhere
The long forgotten food
Filling your hunger and more
The long forgotten . . .

These are the things we remember
As we travel to the home of our past.

The long forgotten house
Offering shelter to new ones living within.
The long forgotten scent of orange blossoms
Shading passageways everywhere.
The long forgotten dessert folk
Teaching us the way of life.

The long forgotten college friends
Having moved away some time ago.
The long forgotten eternal sun,
Burning the land, my skin, my feet.
The long forgotten sycamore
Blooming in spring.
The long forgotten whistle of the train
Pulling through towns
So many times . . .

(Rewrite published in the November 2000 edition of
the Eclectics!)

Save My Man

Knock, knock, there is a knock at the door.
I see a wolf at the forest shore.
He vanishes among the trees.
I quietly close the door with ease
And hear the wolf's begging no more.

Next day, there is a knock at the door.
Again I see the wolf at the forest shore.
He begs and vanishes among the trees.
I hesitate, then close the door.
And heed the wolf's begging no more.

A third day brings a knock at my door.
I see the wolf frantic at the forest shore.
And as he rushes ahead of me
I follow him from tree to tree,
Deep into the forbidden woods.

And there, oh there, I found
The wreckage of a plane on the ground.
And next to it a woman dead
A man beside her,
Barely holding on to life's thread.

We took him out and eased his pain.
We cleaned away the wreckage plane.
I waited next day to come again
And with it a visit from the wolf.
By now an eerie friend.

But—alas—
There was no knock at my door
And the wolf,
The wolf came no more.

(Published in "Spooks, Ghosts, Elves, Fairies, Demons, Monsters, Gods & Goddesses . . . and such," 1996, *Creative with Words Publications*.)

Monterey, California, USA

2003

No specific date other than 2003

My Father's Wants

My father wanted to be a railroad engineer.
He passed this on to me his only son.
But my father's eyes were not strong enough,
So he opted for his second choice to be a forester.
Again, his eyes were not strong enough,
So he became what his father wanted him to be,
An agra-chemist, and when he graduated,
He took his father's money meant for him
And vagabonded around the world.
Twice he circumvented Africa,
Settled in Kenya where his daughters were born;
And then in Europe, where I was born.
One daughter became a forester,
The other a singer, and I became the engineer.
Son and daughters' eyes were not strong enough,
But times had changed.

(Published in the July/August 2004, Vol. 6, *the Eclectics!*)

Monterey, California, USA

2004

July – August 2004

Prisoner of War

Four years earlier she had come
To be a gentleman's farmer's wife,
A philosopher, a writer, a poet,
A story teller of some sort—
A German.

My mother, the sweetest and kindest woman,
With one gavel's blow
Was determined a prisoner of war
To be deported far from British soil,
On which it was believed,
A five foot three inch woman
Could do the country harm.

And as the prison ship left
Mombasa and the Kenyan shore,
My father stood alone
Not knowing that it would be
Eight long years until he was allowed
To see my mother again.

(Based on true facts in the author's family. Published in the July / August 2004 edition of *the Eclectics!*)

If I Had Only One of Them

I was born in a far-off land,
Between the borders of Sudan and Uganda.
On Kenyan soil.
My parents were always around.

I was reared in a household on the European
Continent with most of the family around,
Being the youngest a while, secure and safe.

I started a new life with my father and mother,
My older sister and younger brother
In North America's northern land.

Years later, I was on the move again,
With husband and only son
To the eastern United States, building a home.

Now, I stand in the west alone, wondering
What happened to my homes
In Africa, in Europe, in Canada?

I wish, if I had only one of them.

(Published July / August 2004 *the Eclectics!*)

An Act of Kindness Paid For Dearly

When in South Africa, my father
Collected the pictures for
Our South African Flora and
Our South African Fauna books.

One hundred cards they were each
From the United Tobacco Company
To complete a book for his daughters,
For my sister and for me.

Whether he smoked the merchandise
To do this kindly deed, is not known.
But in old age he suffered.
Emphysema was not kind to him.

With my father gone,
And my sister gone as well
I hold both of the books to my heart.
I hold them dearly and I cry . . .

(Published July / August 2004 *the Eclectics!*)

November – December 2004

Will We Get It Done?

Once again, we try to keep the weather in check,
Hurrying before the rains come and wet down all.
It is repair time around the house!
First the roof, then the eaves,
The downpours, and the gutter grates.
With all of this done, the painter moves in
And strips and strips and strips
The house and garage of many colors.

Flooded are front yard and backyard now.
Piled high debris from every plant
That was nicked and cut to make room
For other plants.
The north side of the house

Is wet and stays wet
For days and weeks to come.

Above in a dark narrow sky,
Clouds circle, gray streaks
On the horizon form.
The fog hangs low.
Will we get it all done before
The rainy season truly is here
For endless months to come?

(Published in "Nature, Seasons, Holidays," November –
December 2004, *Creative with Words Publications*.)

First Thanksgiving

My wife has long been laid to rest,
Long before the children left the nest.
Now all the children are grown and gone.
For the first time, I'll celebrate Thanksgiving alone.
The cat is with me and so is the dog,
In the barn the cow, the horse, the hog.
All six of us will celebrate.
We'll watch TV till it is late.
And eat a grand feast, one to write about home,
Not thinking about it that we're alone.
Happy Thanksgiving, I say a toast to me
And to all my farmyard family.

(Published in "Nature, Seasons, Holidays,"
November – December 2004, *Creative with Words Publications*.)

**Thanksgiving in
Schorndorf, Germany;
photo by the author.**

A Friend Is Gone

She was always there,
Always in the background.
I was never there.

She had given me her name
I knew her well.
I did not give her my name.

She was always loving me
From afar.
I took it for granted.
And then one day

She was gone
And I remembered her love.

I cried,
Not knowing why.
Was it because she was gone?

Or . . .

I never had the time to love her.
I know I was in her heart.
But was she ever in mine?

Monterey, California, USA

2005

April 2005

Her Passing

I read, she passed away,
In the local obit.
Her picture showed her
As she always was,
Full of spirit,
A large brimmed hat,
Covering her smiling face.
I momentarily forgot
To be sad about her passing.
I smiled at the picture
Which portrayed her to me
As I knew her in the past.

(Published in "Mankind," April 2005, *Creative with Words Publications*.)

May – June 2005

When It Rains

When it rains
    I lie in bed, covered up,
      Only my nose peeks out.
When it rains
    I cuddle on a pillow and mat

In front of the fireplace.

When it rains
    I surround myself with books,
    Reading for hours.
When it rains
    I call up work and let them know
    I won't be in.
When it rains
    . . .

(Published in "Seasons, Nature & Animals," May – June 2005, *Creative with Words Publications*.)

October 2005

Second house from left is the one in which the author spent her childhood; photo by the author

What Is It?

What could this be?
Is it a hotel
Or a museum I see?
Is it the one-time home
Of ancestors gone long time ago?
Is it just a house in town,
Which looks smart,
And is well known?

I cannot tell,
Whether it is a museum
Or a spooky hotel
Or an ancestor's home.

(Published in "Folklore," October 2005, *Creative with Words Publications*.)

Monterey, California, USA

(The author traveled with work colleagues to Amman, Jordan, to attend a language conference. While there, her colleagues toured together with her Petra, Aqaba, the Baptismal Site, and the north of Jordan. In September the author retired after having worked for fifty-three years at various universities—Sauk Valley College, University of Arizona, University of California—Berkeley, University of California—Los Angeles—and a language school in Monterey.)

2006

January 2006

The Waterfall

I am the waterfall.
All parts of me are the waterfall.
My hair falls down to my hips
In watery streaks.
My face is the churning top
Where water starts to fall.
My arms stretch out to the sides
Forming rivulet types of falls themselves.
My feet jump to the ground
To merge with a creek.
I am the waterfall.

(Published in the January 2006 edition of *the Eclectics!*)

Waterfall near Bergen,
Norway; photo
by the author.

I Heard the Patter

I heard the patter on the porch,
And then a running on the roof.
There was a lot of clatter
In the backyard around
The water barrels, to be sure.

As I turned on the light,
What did I see?
A group of raccoons
Trying every trick
To open the water-barrel lids.

I opened the window
To shoo them away.
No fear of me,
They stood on their hind legs
Begging me to open the lids.

I filled a water bowl and carried
It to the backyard. Whoosh,
Went one, then the other three.
Next morning, the water bowl
Not empty, stood still full.

(Published in "2006 ~Themes~ 2006," February – March 2006, *Creative with Words Publications*.)

July 2006

The Dead Sea

I am not sure
Why it is called
The Dead Sea.

Is it the salt cresting
Along the shores?
The salty waters
Which keep one afloat?

It is truly a sight
To stand at Jordan's side
Seeing Israel
Lying across the sea.

From the top
Of mountains
One senses
Rising towers of Jerusalem.
So near, yet so far.

September 6, 2006
(The author's retirement date)

I Am Retired!

When I awoke
The first morning
Not having to go to work,
I said to myself,

"No more bosses."
What a great feeling
This was.

Now I Am Free!

When I woke up the first morning
After having worked for many years,
My first reaction was:
No more bosses!
That alone allowed my insides
To jubilate.
I could do what I wanted to do,
For the first time,
I was free!

The View

I have heard that a view is most important,
At a hotel, a restaurant, at work, or at home.
When I purchased the house, I had a view,
A view of the bay!

Every year my view of the bay disappeared more.
No, it was not age to blame or poor eyesight,
It was the growth of trees.
Now, in our town, trees cannot be chopped down.

They stand protected by city law,
But they can be trimmed.
And that is just what happened.
One day, when I came home from work
My view of the bay was restored.

I stood and gazed, holding on to it,
To the view every minute.

Taking in the blue sparkling with white caps,
Before again replaced by spreading green.

(Published in "~Themes~," October 2006, *Creative with Words Publications*.)

November 2006

Miracle at the Lake

Four little cygnets,
Gray in their plumes,
Protected by their parents
That the ducks will not
Snatch away their food.

One cygnet already imitates
Its parents' threat by the ducks.
But it is not a warning hiss,
It is a tiny "Peep!"

(Published in "Animals in Nature . . . With a Touch of Seasons," November 2006, *Creative with Words Publications*.)

Monterey, California, USA

(The author started to travel extensively. Five trips this year: Bermuda, Yucatan, Los Angeles, Canada, and Eastern Europe.)

2007

Izamal, Yucatan, Mexico, Mayan ruin; photo by the author.

No poetry was written.

Monterey, California, USA

(The author traveled to Switzerland, staying at the foot of the Matterhorn, then taking the Glacier Express; with a personal stopover at Lucerne where she went up Mount Pilatus. The author also traveled to the Yucatan to see the Mayan ruins.)

2008

April 2008

Raccoon Family

First came the mother,
Skinny and in need of nutrition.
Then she came with six little ones.
One was limping. It did not make it.

There were six, mother included.
One day, the mother and her five
Met the orphan, now number six,
And they became a family,
All seven of them.

Today they are grown.
Every night it is Halloween at our house.
When they come knocking
Knock, knock, knock at the door,
They ask for food, please.

The loner first,
Then the two girls . . .
The mother and daughter team . . .
And then the five boys.
Rascals, we call them.

Bowls and dishes are flying.
The troop in between
Seven and midnight,
Standing on hind legs,
Begging for more.

And then there is Albert,
The big male.
He has manners.
He eats neatly and precisely.
But he is shy, very shy.

(Published in "Animals & Environment," April 2008, *Creative with Words Publications*.)

We Saw It

We went there
Immediately after we
Arrived early evening
To the church yard
And from there
We saw it
Majestically rise
The Matterhorn.

**The author's first glimpse
of the Matterhorn;
photo by the author.**

Do You See the Star?

Do you see the star in the sky?
    I see it, I see it.
I have never seen such a star before.
    I have never seen it, never seen it.
It points to something here on Earth.
    What could it be, what could it be?
Might it be a stable?
    Like the one in Bethlehem, in Bethlehem?
With the Savior child in a crib?
    In a crib, in a crib.
Let's go toward the star,
    And see what it is, what it is.
And so we went.

(Inspired by a nightly phenomenon one Christmas Eve in Bowling Green, Ohio. Reminiscing a conversation between the author and her husband. Published in "Holidays & Seasons," July 2008, *Creative with Words Publications*.)

The Once Forbidden Mountain

It rose majestically
Besides the city by the lake
Mount Pilatus, that is,
By Lucerne.

When I was there
It was the forbidden mountain.
Why, was not explained.
It just was.

Later I found out that
Possibly Pontius Pilate
Drowned in a lake
On it; it's not clear.

Now the forbidden mountain
Has become unforbidden.
You can travel it
As much as you wish.

Ride to its top,
Hike it,
Take the incline train
The tram, whatever you wish.

(Revisiting Mount Pilatus in Lucerne, Switzerland, Summer 2009.)

**Climbing up the backside of Mount Pilatus
with the cog-wheel rail; photo by the author.**

Monterey, California, USA

(The author went for the first time to Alaska, and then to the Panama Canal. July 3, 2009, the author's aunt, Rose Marie Gaupp, passed away.)

2009

March 2009

I See

I see the sun bursting forth
On a cold wintry day,
And temperatures rise
As in high summer time.

The flowers are confused.
One day to bloom,
The next to seek shelter
From icy winds, blowing south.

Bees hum happy tunes,
Buzzing from blossom to blossom,
Sipping nectar from early plants
Placed on picnic tables.

Birds chirp as little elves
Patter out of tree houses
To putter around the garden,
Trimming back what grew in abundance.

And then . . .
And then it got cold again.

(Published in "The World Is a Fantasy!" March 2009,
Creative with Words Publications.)

July 3, 2009

The Passing of My Aunt

I loved her dearly
My aunt, cousin on Mother's side.
I visited her almost yearly.
She and her house were my pride.

We laughed together
We went out to eat.
It did not matter how the weather
We had fun wherever to meet.

And then one day
I heard the sad news:
My aunt had passed away.

There will be no more
Fun as we had galore.

I at her graveside now stand
With a rose in my trembling hand
And toss it down to her.
Tears follow without end.

My heart breaks.
I know
I will no longer have my aunt
She will be missed for evermore.

(Reminiscent of the passing of Rosemarie Gaupp.)

**Aunt Rose on the balcony
of the little guest house, the
Gütle; photo by the author.**

Monterey, California, USA

(The author went to the North Cape—Nordkapp Municipality—in Norway, and then on a second trip to Antarctica: Chile, Argentina, Antarctica, Falkland Islands, Uruguay, and once again Argentina. The author's back was in a serious state of health and needed surgery. The author had to do much of her travel in a wheelchair.)

2010

February 20, 2010

Where Has Our Castle Gone?

Where has our castle gone?
It is nowhere to be found.
We came from northern
European shores
To England, and after that
Were for Ireland bound.

For centuries we dwelled there.
And when one of the famines came
To Switzerland, we moved,
Building a house there, a town,
Moved to Lake Constance's shores.
There a castle we built.

Proud and high it stood.
Our righteousness
Gave honor to us
And Ferdinand the Second
Opened our helmet.

We had become aristocracy!

Forever we would be . . .

Today, the castle is nowhere,
Just a few rocks, nothing more,
And a town
Which bears our name.

Only the crest
Hanging on our wall tells
Of a glory long time gone by.

(In memory of Sigmarshofen, Germany, south of Ravensburg.)

Monterey, California, USA

(The author had back surgery and was recuperating in a convalescent home for those who had no one at home to take care of them. Outside the author's window was the statue of Dr. Dalton. Once the author was in better shape, she went on a second trip, a sea and land trip, to Alaska, and to Brazil to travel along the Amazon.)

2011

No specific date other than 2011

The Doctor in the Park
(Dedicated to Dr. Dalton.)

Among oaks he sits in life-size stature
Easy in rest, eyes looking out
Over the peninsula beyond the trees.
Years ago, he served the town,
Today he sits on a wooden bench.
In rain, in wind, in sunshine, in storm—yet
Day and night in comfort
In his corduroy pants and jacket,
Below balconies of the dwelling,
Where people come seeking health.

An aura of peace surrounds him,
Great tranquility,
Among jays, black and blue,
And squirrels large with gray-ruffled tails,
Playing from branch to branch,
At times resting beside him
On the bench's edge or on him,
Keeping him company.

(Published in "Tumble," 2012, *Creative with Words Publications*.)

Monterey, California, USA

(The author traveled by the riverboat *Avalon* from Amsterdam to the Black Sea. Within two weeks of that trip, the author went from Amsterdam to Svalbard/ Spitzbergen, the Nordic ice, Iceland, Faroe Islands—an archipelago between the Norwegian Sea and the North Atlantic—, Scotland, and back to Amsterdam.)

2013

No specific date other than 2013

To Pen and Paper

To pen and paper
I took
And rewrote
Stories of long ago:

Tales to my child,
Stories, when I grew up,
And novels always in the making,
Never being completed.

There was no longer time
For writing poetry.
So, I sat down and wrote
And wrote and wrote.
I wrote prose.

Will This Be Our Future?

What is it we need to exist in this world
For a long time, if not for eternity?
Will we only need a head
That distinguishes us from one another
And the rest of our bodies
Will be computerized,
Mechanical components?
Think about it!
It is possible.

(Published in the February/March 2013 edition of *the Eclectics!*)

Monterey, California, USA

(The author traveled to Greece, Turkey, through the Black Sea, and back to Greece.)

2014

No poetry was written.

Monterey, California, USA

(The author traveled from Dover, England, to Lisbon, Portugal, and from Lisbon, Portugal, to Rome, Italy. She had a chance to visit Gibraltar. On her second voyage the author traveled from Greece to the Holy Land, Israel, to Rome, Italy, and from Rome, Italy, to Fort Lauderdale, Florida, USA, as the ship repositioned from the old world to the new world.)

2015

Rain!

I felt it,
I smelled it,
We needed it,
To feed the dry land,
The yards and fields,
The thirsty ones.

A pleasure,
A treasure
From the sky.
We take it,
We make it
A blessing
From God
In disguise.

(Published in "Nature . . . " 1998, *Creative with Words Publications*.)

June 21

The author's former husband and friend passed away

Dr. Douglas George Pierce Junior Ludgate and his cat Meggie; photo by a friend

October 2015

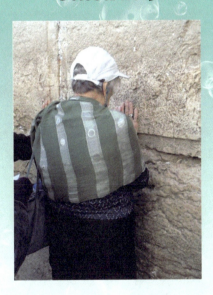

The author at the Wailing Wall; photo taken by the author's friend Philo Pisters of the Netherlands

At the Wailing Wall

I said a prayer,
A Christian prayer,
For I am not Jewish,
Thinking of the pope,
Having done the same.

I said a prayer
Thanking God for everything.
My life has been great,
My friends are few but true.

And my son . . .
My son was talking to me again.
I said a prayer . . .

Monterey, California, USA

(The author went for a third time to Alaska to visit the Russian cities; unfortunately, a severe storm kept her from doing so, and the ship was redirected to Skagway for the author to visit the Yukon instead.)

2016

No specific date other than early 2016

There Is Love

There is love,
Many kinds of love.
Love between a man
And a woman;
Love between a parent
And a child.
But there is also love,
When Grandma puts her arms
Around you and smiles.

(Inspired by a photograph of Omi Wassermann
hugging the author's brother, Klaus-Peter, at a younger age.)

Grandma Wassermann cuddles Klaus-Peter; photo by a family member.

The Cat and She Needed Gas

She stood there, at the side of the road,
Holding a sign, telling drivers coming by,
She needed gas.
Now, that was something new.
It had us drivers puzzled.

She stood, well-dressed,
The dog at her side,
Well-groomed, well-mannered,
But the sign in her hand said,
She needed gas.

I drove past her, wondering
Will anyone respond to her plea?
Give her the money she needed,
Tank up the car for her? After all,
The sign said, she needed gas.

I watched. It did not happen.
Cars sped by her, one by one,
Drivers chuckling, just I had done.
It must have been a joke.
But the sign said, she needed gas.

He stood there at the side of the road,
No sign, just a cat on a leash,
Sitting on his shoulder.
Cars stopped and handed him
A dollar here, and a dollar there.

From a Crow's Point of View

I am a pigeon too.
What do you mean, I'm not?
I come to the feeding trough
Just like you
Early ev'ry morning,
Not just for the peanuts
Which everyone in my family eats,
And those of the blue jays,

And the stellar jays,
And the titmice.
I come for the birdseeds,
Which you like to eat,
And I peck, and I peck, and I peck
Along with you.

April 2016

Running Feet

There are feet running on my roof,
Rather fast, tiny feet.
I do not know whose feet they are.
They are running, running fast.

When I go outside
There is no one with little feet
Running fast on my roof.
But when I'm inside, I hear them
Running fast those tiny feet.

Whose little feet are they?

July 2016

Told Years Later

For a long time I had no father
To hold me, to cuddle me, to love me.
All in my mind,
I saw in every male my father
Whether it was an uncle, a movie star,
A television star,
Or a man on the street.

My friend had no father.
She lost him in Russia
During World War II.
She told me, she saw in my father
Her father
I was wondering whether
He held her, cuddled her, loved her,
All in her mind?

And the Bird Died

It used to sit on the wire
Across the street
From the house which stood
Securely fenced in.

It used to fly across the street
To the house securely fenced in
To meet with its own kind,
To peck at morsels spread there.

It used to coo,
It used to walk behind
Female birds
With mating on its mind.

And now it sits in the sun
Needing its warmth
As it can no longer fly
From the house securely fenced in.

And the sun warmed it
Its body lapping up every beam
And then it stood there motionless
Waiting . . .

It waited for death to come.
And its legs could no longer
Hold it and it sank to the ground.
. . .
The bird had died.

A Storm at Sea

A storm at sea, came on suddenly,
We were in Anchorage, Alaska, to see
The land and the ice.
Next day excursions would be
To former Russian sites:
Homer, Kodiak, Sitka, and
The Hubbard Glaciers.

Gale force winds roared,
Stirring up the Alaskan Bay
And with it Cook's Inlet.
The captain had to decide
Where to seek shelter
For passengers and crew.

And excursions to three Russian sites
Were stricken: Homer, Kodiak, and Sitka.
And a cruising past the Hubbard Glacier.
And the captain steered the ship
Quickly toward the Inside Passage,
To seek shelter there.

What a disappointment.
But . . .
But the Yukon was calling us
From Skagway.

Drought

Oh how sad,
The rains had not come
Another year of scorching sun.
The plants in my yard have died
And those which did not
The deer feasted on.
Now the plants are dead.
They will no longer grow.
And we had to pull them
Out of the ground,
One by one.
The yard is bare . . . .

Monterey, California, USA

(The author went to Ireland to visit the home of her presumable ancestors north of Ennis at the west coast. It was stormy, and she did not get to Ennis and instead she went to Glasgow, Scotland, and Belfast, Northern Ireland.)

2017

March 2017

Drought and Flood

My garden and yard
Blooms and bushes grow
In a furious mass this year.
Plants pushing forth
And so do
Shrubs and trees.
Flowers blossom everywhere
In total confusion.

It was not always like that.
Just a year ago, all had died,
Or so it seemed.

The drought took its toll.
Shrubs had to be torn down,
Trees had to be taken out,
Plants did not grow
Nor did they bloom.
And then, this year . . .
This year the rains came.

The rains came in abundance.
They came, and they came
And they came.

Now everything grows,
Stretching out toward the sky,
Stretching out toward the sun,
Stretching out from the front
To the back.
Stretching out everywhere.

I do not have the heart
To cut anything back.
But I have to,
Sooner or later.

Everything grows
In utter profusion
Here and there and everywhere.
Until the time comes when
I have to get to them with
Scissors and shears
And start to cut back the abundance.

April 10, 2017

Flower in Early Spring

A plant has brought forth
A bud so tiny and so fine.
It's still bent, not opened up
In early spring time.

It is pink now
I can see.

But soon, it will be red
When the time comes
For it to be.

A plant has brought forth
A bud so tiny and so fine.

A Little Bird, an Animal, a Neighbor

A little bird came flying to my house.
It chirped about the situation in the world.
It is not as good as once it was.
What can be done?

A little animal came running to my house.
Informing me about the sad things
Happening everywhere.
What can be done?

A neighbor came walking up to my house,
Frightened about everything
Going on in the world.
It is no longer a safe place to live.

What can we do?

We can love each other,
The good and the not-so-good,
The extremely wicked ones.
Maybe then, maybe then . . .

No little bird or animal
Or my neighbor needs to come
To my house,
Concerned, worried, frightened.
Because all will be good.

April 25, 2017

Werner Gugelmeier, cousin of the author; the family connection goes back to
Oberkirch in the Black Forest, Germany; photo taken by unknown

My Cousin and I

Cousin that is what you are.
Second-degree cousin,
Or is it third or fourth?
Born the same year as I.
And we wrote to one another
Year-in, year-out.

Sharing our thoughts,
Sharing our deeds.
You living afar,
I am living here.

You were married twice.
I was married once.
You have a daughter.
I have a son.

We grew old together,
The only ones of our age
Still around, so it seems.
And now we walk together
In our minds, hand in hand.

We walk toward a setting sun,
Just down the road ahead of us.

May 2017

So Cold!

It was cold,
Very cold.
My parka's hood
Firmly pressed up to my eyes,
A scarf tight around the hood
To keep it there
From blowing off.

It was July,
This earth can
Truly be cold,
Very cold.
Maybe I need to move
To somewhere else,
Where it is warm
All of the time.

May 11, 2017

May, May!

May, May,
Beautiful May!
The first month
Of the year
Without an *r* in its name.

Now I can sit on the ground,
Touching the soil,
The grass,
The flowers in bloom.

Loving all
Without the fear
Of winter months
Giving me the chill.

Extraditing

My father was Mexican,
My mother, I do not know.
My father came to America
A long time ago.

My father is a kind man,
A man full of caring heart.
He is not an American
And soon he has to part.

I was born in America,
A U.S. citizen I am.
My father has to leave this land.
And I?
Where do I stand?

(Inspired by current rumors that all noncitizens of the United States will have to be deported.)

May 26, 2017

Zebras Out in the Savanna

Out in the savanna
Where zebras roam
And the lions roar,
Where by the lake they meet,
And elephants ramble,
And so do crocodiles,

There stands a hut
With a swinging door.
The woman lies shivering
Fearing what might come more.
The husband laughs
And turns to his side.
"Even if the door is locked,"
He says,
"One shove with the paw and
The animal will be inside."

(Reminiscent of a story the author's mother told, brought back to the author by a documentary of zebras in Africa.)

June 1, 2017

I Remember . . .

I remember airports,
Kennedy for instance,
Known as Idlewild
In New York,
Where I and my friends
Leaned over a fence
Watching foreigners alight.

Then I remember that LA
Had an airport
On the other side,
Long before Tom Bradley's,
And if you were in a hurry
And came to the wrong airport
You most likely missed your flight.

I remember
When with child
And with cat and with dog
I traveled to Monterey,
We almost filled
The entire plane.

I remember . . .
But now it's different.

June 25, 2017

Went Swimming

Spencer and I went swimming
Out in the ocean, out at sea.
He was splashing in crested waters,
I lay in the sun, absorbing the heat.

Spencer and I went swimming.

(The author reminiscing when she and her son went swimming year-round at the beaches of Santa Monica, California.)

August 2, 2017

An extinct flower still blooming in the author's yard; photo by the author

Whenever . . .

Whenever I see the green,
I smell the juicy grass,
Full of dew drops.

Whenever I see the color
Of a rose so full in bloom,
I smell the scent of its blossoms.

Whenever I hear the song
Of a bird jubilating out loud,
I feel like standing below it.

Whenever I hear the rushing
Of the waves,
I see fish and seals and much more.

Whenever I hear a group of children
Imitating the calls and the deeds
Of their elders, I am not there.

Whenever . . .

I smell nothing,
I see nothing,
I hear nothing.

Everything is a picture in my dark mind
For I am housebound
And I cannot see or hear
Or get out of my bed.

No Date Given

Poem

If I could stay up on the rocks
The highest point and nearest to God,
I would stay there
In rain and in fog
And in beautiful sunshine.

If I could not stay up on the rocks
The highest point and nearest to God,
I would not know where to stay
In rain and in fog
And in beautiful sunshine.

Flying over the Clouds

As I flew over the clouds
I passed so many sites
I once called home
Or at least
I traveled to them
As temporary home.

First there was LA,
Where I dwelled for years
And studied for a degree.
Knowing that my son
Still lives there
Made my heart sing.
Knowing that my friend
Was no longer there,
Made my heart weep.

And then there was
Illinois and Detroit,
And on the Canadian side
There was Sarnia
And Wallaceburg . . .

(Poem is incomplete. There is no date given when it was written.)

August 10, 2017

Fleeting Years

And so the years go by,
One faster than the previous one.
Hardly is Christmas and New Year's over
As it is once again end of August,

And with it fall knocks on the door.
Where does the time go? I ask.
No one has an answer for me.
It just went.

I Slept on an Island

I slept on an island,
Bon Aire was its name,
It belonged to the father
Of my beloved man.

We got there by rowboat,
The dog with us.
He loved to roam the island
When we were there or not.

The lake roared at times
In the middle of the night,
The waves rushing back and forth,
And the wind blew
And we had a fire
In the fireplace
And oil lamps everywhere
To light up the house.

I slept on an island
In the arms of my beloved man.
Today he is gone
And the island for me is no more.

Bon Aire, **Georgian Bay, the
Ludgate cabin; photo by the author.**

(Reminiscent of *Bon Aire*, the island in Georgian Bay belonging to Douglas John Ludgate, the father of the author's husband, Douglas George Pierce Junior Ludgate.)

The Fence

The fence has saved my plants,
The growth in my yard.
The deer stay out
And do not eat the blossoms
And the plants stand full in bloom.

The hummingbirds are back
Dipping their beaks
Into blue and white petals
Of Nile lilies,
And fertilize the plants.

And the bees come again
And hum in their buzz
They are everywhere
As well.

The fence has saved my plants,
The growth in my yard.
Until . . .
Until the young buck jumps the fence.

(Observation by the author of the return of hummingbirds and bees.)

September 3, 2017

The Screeching Gulls

Eager screeches of gulls,
Awakening barks of sea lions,

V-shaped flocks of geese,
Forlorn warning of a lighthouse horn,
The tooting of a pilot ship
Below the Golden Gate Bridge,
Soundly response
By the sleek cruise ship . . .

These are the sounds
Of entering San Francisco harbor
Early in the morning,
Long before the city emerges
Out of daily fog banks,
Welcoming travelers home
From their journey abroad.

(Written some time earlier; however, no date is available.)

September 19, 2017

It Does Not Matter

"I am the faster one,"
Called the river to the other river
Flowing nearby.
"You will see,
I'll get to the ocean
Long before you do."
"No," called the other river
Across the open land.
"I am much faster than you."

"I have the clearest water,"
Said the river coming closer

To the other river.
"No," said the other river.
"My water is the clearest."

"I am pure through and through
All the way,"
Murmured the first river.
"Not as pure as I am,"
Murmured the second river.

Both lost sight
In their travel through the land,
And . . .

Oops!

Each in its own way
Down it tumbled
In beautiful waterfalls
Side by side
And below.
They emerged as one.

September 22, 2017

High Summer

We had high summer this year,
Not in October as usual,
But in September.
It was extremely hot
And almost all of our houses
Have no air conditioning.
The hardware store sold

Over seventy fans on one day.
I had the icebox door open
To get some coolness into the house.
The thermometer said
It was one hundred and one
For almost three days.

It is now
Cooling down a bit.

October 3, 2017

Visiting a Friend

Here I sit
In the hospital.
A friend of mine
Had surgery.
I hope she will
Be well soon.

The doctors
Are making their rounds.

It is not time yet
To go into the room
To visit.
But I know
Soon I will hug her
And hold her hand.

The end of "Poetry through a Lifetime,

Part II," the later years.

List of Poetry included in the publication *Stepping Through Time*, written by the author and published May 12, 2014

Poetry in *Stepping Through Time*

External Time

   From Age to Age:

      High Dreams . . . Low Reward

      Evolution

      Homo's Dilemma

      A Candita: Wheels . . .

      Page of Life

      Perennial Search

      Perennial Question

      Tell Us

      Fears

      The Future and the Present

      The Corn God Is Coming

      Bonifacius!

      San Geronimo Dashers (September 30)

      Fleeting Trickster

      In Times of Great Doubt

      Gold of Heaven

      Knowing Not

      Southwestern Survey

      The Same

      Loss

      Call Upon Sebasteion

      On the Passing of Temple Statues

      Give or Take

      Quest for Change

      King Arthur at the Bay

      In Control of the Sun

Books
by the Author

Books by the Author

Brigitta Gisella Geltrich-Ludgate

Geltrich von Sigmarshofen, in memory of the author's father, Rudolf Karl Geldreich
1904 – 1981
(published by Creative with Words Publications, 1985)

Ruth Margarete Geldreich, née Boehnke, in memory of the author's
mother, Ruth Margarete Geldreich, née Boehnke
1910 – 1989
(published by Creative with Words Publications, 1994)

Gold Child Urle: Ursula Ingrid Kristensen, née Geldreich, 1935 – 2001, in memory of the
author's sister
(published by Creative with Words Publications, 2001)

Tales and Bedtime Stories
(published January 18, 2013, by Xlibris)
Library of Congress Control Number: 2012923853

The Muddy Little Bell
(published May 9, 2013, by Xlibris)
Library of Congress Control Number: 2013905477

The Lucia Rider
(published November 18, 2013, by Xlibris)
Library of Congress Control Number: 2013918730

Stepping through Time
(published May 12, 2014, by Xlibris)
Library of Congress Control Number: 2014906340

Fathers Can Be Good Dads
(published September 25, 2014, by Xlibris)
Library of Congress Control Number: 2014914297

Dance around the Treasure Box
(published February 20, 2015, by Xlibris)
Library of Congress Control Number: 2015901808

Two Summers of Adjustment
(published December 28, 2015, by Xlibris)
Library of Congress Control Number: 2015921174

The Little People of Oakcreek
(published April 23, 2016, by Xlibris)
Library of Congress Control Number: 2016906328

Cindy the Balcony Cocoon
(published May 27, 2016, by Xlibris)
Library of Congress Control Number: 2016908513

Out of Balance
(published October 27, 2016, by Xlibris)
Library of Congress Control Number: 2016915352

Stories, Tales, Folklore, and Such As!
(published March 24, 2017, by Xlibris)
Library of Congress Control Number: 2017900063

I Am Jet, Jet the Cat
(published April 6, 2017, by Xlibris)
Library of Congress Control Number: 2017904990

Gedichte eines Lebens (Poetry through a Lifetime)
Part I: Early Years (with English translations by the author)
(published August 23, 2017, by AuthorHouse)
Library of Congress Control Number: 2017911409

Poetry through a Lifetime
Part II: Later Years
(published by AuthorHouse)

The author is currently finishing up her novel "Moving to Alaska." Still to be published are the two volumes of "There Were Many of Us on Three Continents—Memoirs of Brigitta Gisella Geltrich-Ludgate and Her Family."